To Danelle Nash
with best regards

Sincerely Reagan

Love
you

Franky Regan

Also in the Great Restaurants of the World series:

Charlie Trotter's
Commander's Palace
The Inn at Little Washington
The Sardine Factory

An Insider's Look at the Famed Restaurant and Its Cuisine

Fred Ferretti

Photographs by Mick Hales

Lebhar-Friedman Books

New York • Chicago • Los Angeles • London • Paris • Tokyo

Lebhar-Friedman Books
425 Park Avenue
New York, NY 10022

Published by Lebhar-Friedman Books
Lebhar-Friedman Books is a company of Lebhar-Friedman, Inc.

Great Restaurants of the World® is a trademark
of Lebhar-Friedman Books.

Printed in the United States of America

Library of Congress Cataloging-in-Publication Data

Ferretti, Fred
    Café des Artistes : an insider's look at the famed restaurant
and its cuisine / Fred Ferretti
        p. cm. — (Great restaurants of the world)
    ISBN 0-86730-801-X (alk. paper)
    1. Café des Artistes (New York, N.Y.) 2. Lang, George, 1924-
    3. Cookery, International I. Cafe des Artistes (New York, N.Y.)
II. Title III. Series.

    TX945.5.C27 F47 2000
    641.5'09747'1—dc21
                                                        99-059968

Book design: Nancy Koch, NK Design

An SCI production

Jacket design: Kevin Hanek
Photographs © 2000 by Mick Hales

Visit our Web site at lfbooks.com

About the author

Fred Ferretti, long an observer and critic of the food and restaurant worlds, is a contributing editor at *Gourmet* and creator of that magazine's column "A Gourmet at Large." A journalist and writer who has been a political and social reporter, columnist, critic, correspondent, and producer for *The New York Herald Tribune, NBC-TV News,* and *The New York Times,* he has written for virtually every major magazine in the United States. He is author of four previous books: *The Great American Marble Book* and *The Great American Book of Sidewalk, Street, Dirt, Curb, and Alley Games,* both books of nostalgia; *Afo-A-Kom: Sacred Art of Cameroon,* a study of an aspect of African art; and *The Year the Big Apple Went Bust,* a political case study of New York's flirtation with bankruptcy.

In recognition of the body of his work, particularly in the field of gastronomy, Ferretti was made a Chevalier of the Republic of Italy in 1979 and a Knight of the Kingdom of Belgium in 1989. He is an *officier* of the prestigious Ordre des Coteaux de Champagne, as well as a member of other wine and food societies. Ferretti is married to Eileen Yin-Fei Lo, the celebrated author of many books on the cookery of China. The couple live in Montclair, New Jersey, and have three children.

About the photographer

Mick Hales is one of America's foremost interior and garden photographers. His work is published as sole photographer in 11 books and appears in numerous magazines. Currently, he is writing and photographing a book on monastic gardens. He lives with his wife, painter Christine Simoneau, in New York's Hudson Valley.

CONTENTS

FOREWORD

Few experiences in life enhance the joy of living more than a fine dining experience. The ambience, style, service, food, and presentation of a great restaurant are all elements that add immensely to enjoying a culinary adventure. Many restaurants provide customers with a consistent dining experience, and a number of these are truly outstanding. Only a few, however, exceed the expectations of even their most discerning patrons. They deserve to be called great, and we are proud to recognize them as Great Restaurants of the World. The first five restaurants in this series of books are:

Café des Artistes
Charlie Trotter's
Commander's Palace
The Inn at Little Washington
The Sardine Factory

These beautiful books have been a labor of love and dedication for all the parties involved. We have called upon the editors of *Nation's Restaurant News,* the leading business publication serving the restaurant industry, to assist us in developing the criteria for the Great Restaurants of the World series and in choosing the candidates. We think you will agree that the selections are of great interest and merit.

All of the Great Restaurants of the World represent a unique creative spirit of providing the public with a meaningful dining experience. However, they also share many of the same traits. Most significantly, each was founded by one or more persons with the kind of entrepreneurial energy dedicated to achieving excellence. Without exception, these founders instilled in their organizations a single compelling mission: to provide their guests with the ultimate dining experience. Food and food presentation are always the first priority. After that come service, ambience, and value.

All of these restaurants have been successful by paying attention to innumerable small details every day, every week, and every month throughout the year. Each has proved, many times over, its reputation as a truly great restaurant through the loyalty of its repeat customers and the steady stream of awards and recognition it has received over the years, both from its guests and from its peers.

This book and the others in the series are your invitation to experience the Great Restaurants of the World, their history and their heritage. Savor every page, and enjoy the adventure.

James C. Doherty
Executive Vice President
Lebhar-Friedman, Inc.

George Lang has been welcoming diners to the Café des Artistes since 1975.

Café des Artistes

AN INTRODUCTORY WORD

Various people can relate bits and pieces about the early days of the Café des Artistes, during its first half century plus, but ours is a personal perspective. As its proprietors since 1975, we can impart with authority the significance of the restaurant that has become so much a part of our lives.

Jenifer: "In the spring of that year, George received a phone call from a member of the board of directors of the Hotel des Artistes, located on the street where we live. The board member asked if George would be interested in taking over the Café.

"I recall George saying he was quite satisfied, thank you, with his personal think tank, developing restaurants and retail complexes around the world for other people. He explained that he did not want to return to restaurant operations in what he considered 'an era of steady disintegration of workmanship and pride,' especially with a dark, dingy little place at the entrance to an apartment house. He further noted that the restaurant was empty most of the time, despite the fact that nearby Lincoln Center was already more than a decade old. So he declined, quoting Mark Twain's observation about the man who was to be tarred, feathered, and ridden out of town: 'If it weren't for the honor, I'd rather walk.'

"A change of heart soon followed. A couple of nights later, George was waiting for a taxi on our block. It was raining and, as usual, no taxis were available. George said, 'If we had a successful restaurant on this block, we could always find a taxi.' The next day he called the board member back and, without having gone through the careful feasibility studies that should precede such decisions, told him, 'I'll take it.' So much for resolve."

George: "What sort of restaurant should the 'new' Café des Artistes be? was a question I pondered and later shared with Jenifer. As I usually do when I have to reckon with the future, I took another look at the past, especially because I knew that none of the then current restaurant fashions would be right. An important part of the heritage of the Café des Artistes is that, over the years, artists lived and worked in virtually all of the buildings along West 67th Street. A highly colorful group who enjoyed their own, occasionally odd, company in their nonworking moments, these creative individuals indulged themselves in interesting, sociable ways.

"The Café was a meeting place for this colony of artists, offering reasonably priced food and, of course, good conversation. What is now our office, on the same block as the Café, served for a couple of decades, beginning in 1905, as a small restaurant-club for the artists living nearby. Both this space and later the Café were fashioned after the English ordinary, a bistro with a menu limited to foods available at the markets.

"Tradition is often a form of conspiracy to hold back change, but adapting this old-fashioned concept to the current market served the Café well. It was not a lofty, Grande Cuisine we were aspiring to create, nor its many strange and faddish offshoots. We sought a cuisine with the flavor and texture of a neighborhood restaurant where good middle-class food—typical French Sunday dinners—would be rounded out by some 'if only I could have' dishes. Our goal, which we believe has

*Jenifer Lang can often be found
greeting the Café's customers.*

been successfully realized, was to re-create the warmth of a Middle European coffeehouse-restaurant—the type of place only occasionally left by the habitués for brief visits to their homes before a hasty return to their *Stammtisch*, their regular tables.

The Café's busy bar offers complimentary quail's eggs (left) and a chance to relax in the warm embrace of a New York landmark.

"Our initial concept excluded foods that are the characteristic symbols of elegance or expense accounts, such as truffles or caviar. Even now, we serve caviar only once each year, at the black-tie New Year's Eve dinner. We were determined to introduce honest dishes of the *cuisine bourgeoise*, to pay special attention to 'mother love' items like bread, butter, and coffee or brewed tea served in double pots. We make our own chutneys, smoke our own fish and seafood, prepare a large variety of traditional charcuteries, and offer a good selection of fresh fruits.

"The world is full of would-be wine connoisseurs who are waiting for the opportunity to say, 'This is a withered wine with discipline and forceful finesse, but [there is usually a pause here, for effect] it is also fierce and succulent.' The restau-

rant world is also full of meaningless wine lists that complicate the simple pleasures of choosing a wine. At the Café, wines are brought up from the cellar in wine baskets, each containing a changing array of red and white wines, all for the same modest price. We also offer a limited selection of 'celebration wines' chosen at our periodic tastings.

"Although brunch has existed for at least 75 years, most probably as a late, or second, breakfast—a *dejeuner à la fourchette*—it became popular in the United States only in the early 1960s. As Restaurant Associates' project director for the Tower Suite, I was part of this brunch revolution. The Tower Suite, on top of the Time-Life Building in midtown Manhattan, customarily served 500 to 600 elegant five-course brunches every Sunday. When we took over the Café, we saw that it was time to bring brunches out of the 'If it's Sunday noon, it must be time for a Bloody Mary and omelette' syndrome. So we chose to open on Saturday and Sunday afternoons. The Café became, it was said, the place to drink the best apricot sour, spread your marrow from the accompanying pot-au-feu on your toast, have your smoked salmon Benedict, read the out-of-town newspapers, and celebrate the fact that you were spending the weekend in the greatest city in the world.

"In an era long past, Maurice Maeterlinck, Isadora Duncan, Alexander Woollcott, and Mayor Fiorello LaGuardia, New York's legendary and beloved 'Little Flower,' had their regular tables in the Café. Now at these tables sit James Levine, Itzhak Perlman and neighbor Kathleen Turner, Frank McCourt, David Halberstam, Ronald Lauder, Robert Caro, E. L. Doctorow, and Richard Holbrook, as well as magazine and newspaper editors, Parisian chefs, restaurateurs, and anyone else passionate about good conversation, honest wine, and food that satisfies.

"Seeing to the comfort of these guests, shepherding the Café's staff, smoothing and arranging everything from linens to pâtés with style, aplomb, and an uncanny, innate culinary knowledge is left in the hands of Jenifer.

"On occasion, when we pass by the small portrait of Howard Chandler Christy gazing around the Café des Artistes from behind table number 38, we suggest to each other that Christy, a man known to be a connoisseur of good wine and beautiful women, is as pleased with it all as we are."

Chef Thomas Ferlesch lavishes careful attention on the Café's singular cuisine.

George Lang

Jenifer Lang

Café des Artistes

CHAPTER ONE

A COZY NICHE IN NEW YORK CITY

A great restaurant should be daily theater, a subtly changing, ever-fresh performance that embraces and involves its customers with warmth and recognition. Food should, while current, retain the comforting familiarity of tradition. Great restaurants welcome. They do not intimidate. Never do they urge patrons overtly to return. Rather, continuity, proficiency, and amity create a palpable aura that simply makes people want to come back.

The Café des Artistes is such a restaurant, a small and most inviting bistro of European inspiration on the western fringe of New York City's Central Park. It is that rarity among restaurants in these trend-sodden United States: a place of permanence, with a juicy gastronomic, artistic, and occasionally raffish history that stretches back more than eight decades. It can be a respite from the urban turmoil of the city that surrounds it, an eating place layered with years that conjures up the coffee-house restaurants of Vienna, Budapest, or Paris. One does not merely dine at the Café des Artistes, one becomes immersed in it—its past, its muted colors, the bounty of its food (baked, steamed, poached, and raw) its aromas, and in the hushed murmur of its conversational buzz, the only noise.

The essence of the Café des Artistes is its past. Above it, around it, and up and down its West 67th Street block lived an artistic community. For much of the last century, and to

One does not merely dine at the Café des Artistes, one becomes immersed in it—its past, its muted colors, and the bounty of its food.

this day, painters and etchers, essayists and novelists, composers and dancers, musicians and journalists lived and worked on the block. They were neighbors, colleagues, often competitors, just as often collaborators. Most of all they were clubbish, and through all of its years the Café has been their community meeting place.

"It was important to keep this past in mind when the Café was reborn in 1975," says George Lang, owner of the Café des Artistes and a restaurant consultant who minds not at all being referred to as a gastronomic impresario. "This block was where a creative intelligentsia worked and lived. These people did not need a glittering showcase to see or be seen in. They, and over the years their successors, wanted a comfortable European dining room, an extension of the home, a place to eat a Sunday dinner in comfort without the more obvious trappings of restaurant elegance. By which I mean caviar, flaming dishes of any kind, and prepared foods that must be boned tableside, that sort of thing."

It was important, says Lang, that the Café "have classic service and a maître d'hôtel, but that it would never dream of wearing either a tux or tails. It would have to be casual, yet proper."

Most of the waitstaff dress in black vests and ankle-length white aprons; others wear full-length green aprons. They have been trained to make customers "feel that

Old-world touches can be found throughout the Café.

Servers, says George Lang, are trained to make customers "feel that they have entered a friendly little island and are welcome."

they have entered a friendly little island and are welcome," says Lang. "If they cannot do that, I tell them, they should instead be ticket-takers at a public swimming pool."

This philosophy has been carried over onto the Café's menu, as well. "Considerably before the current trend toward home-style or comfort foods, which have come to be culinary clichés, the Café served pot-au-feu, *boeuf à la mode,* cassoulet, roast goose, *brandade, bourrides* carefully made pâtés and terrines, and other charcuterie," says Lang. "I added stuffed goose neck, just as my mother cooked it in Hungary, and even my mother's flourless chocolate torte." Ilona Torte, named for Lang's mother and his late daughter, Andrea Ilona, is served throughout the United States under many different names.

The inspiration for its food, and its essential style, have not changed in the quarter-century that Lang has owned the Café des Artistes, a time during which he was joined by his wife, Jenifer, as managing director. "Consistency, consistency," says Lang. "Jenifer watches over the pot-au-feu, for instance. It is exactly the same each time it is served. The same bone, set upright on the plate the same way, the same broth, the marrow spoon set down the same way, the same flavors, served with the same condiments." The Café's chef, Thomas Ferlesch, Vienna born and trained, sees to the classic simplicity of these and other traditional foods issuing from the restaurant's kitchen. "I believe," he says, "in real food."

Warmth, sincerity of greeting, and an anticipation by customers of ease and comfort combine with foods sharing the provenance of the French and European bistro and the familiarity of the home kitchen to make the Café des Artistes one of the most successful restaurants in the United States. With a capacity of 116, it regularly serves between 250 and 300 dinners per evening. Returning guests, and there are a great many, often ask to be served by particular waiters.

A WARM WELCOME

*W*e try to accommodate," says Jenifer Lang, reciting the Café's philosophy. Accommodation takes many forms. There are spare jackets, required at dinner, should men arrive without them, but there is also a collection of eyeglasses for diners who may have forgotten theirs and need to scan the *carte*. People eating alone at the Café des Artistes, particularly women, are given small extra tastes, perhaps an *amuse-gueule* or two, perhaps a complimentary glass of wine, "to give them ease, to make their visit more pleasurable," Jenifer says.

It is also a practice that when a half-dozen oysters are ordered, seven are served, a gesture that always induces a smile of pleasure. It also creates a memory.

All of these caring, visible, and tangible instances of welcome are meant to invite, to please, to be manifestations of the restaurant's philosophy. There is an air of clubbiness about the Café, yet it does not exclude. It welcomes, with quiet but dramatic colors, plantings, lighting, and aromas, all administered by a helpful, knowledgeable staff that complements competence with care and good fellowship.

Customers enjoy the Café's congenial ambience, especially in the cozy Christy Room (right).

To step into the Café des Artistes is to be enveloped in carefully conceived comfort. Its exterior is a series of carved granite Gothic arches framing leaded windows. A flower box dense with English ivy sits at the base of each window. The entrance, through the marbled lobby of the Hotel des Artistes, is flanked by chiseled Gothic carvings that would not be out of place on a chapel in the Loire.

Inside, past the reception desk blooming with a small box of flowers accompanied by sprouting oregano and basil, is a subdued room. The wood paneling and ceiling beams are painted an unobtrusive chocolate brown, an "honest brown," says George Lang. They meld perfectly with the rich glowing forest green of the woven fabric on the banquettes and the more subdued green of the carpeting. The furniture is restaurant-basic: varnished chairs with rounded backs and bentwood frames, tables dressed with white cotton linens into which a fleur-de-lis pattern is woven. Those walls not covered by Howard Chandler Christy's murals of lithesome and supple female nudes are mirrored and highlighted by 70-year-old bronze sconces.

The centerpiece of this front room is a wide, highly polished baker's table supporting a daily tableau of abundance. An urn of multicolored flowers, arranged by floral designer Dennis Cremmins, is surrounded by huge loaves of black and brown bread, bowls of red and yellow peppers, or purple eggplants, or heads of green Savoy cabbage, or deeper green broccoli. There may be a platter of glowing red and yellow tomatoes, interspersed with small green jalapeños. Cruets of oils and vinegars sit alongside an iced bowl filled with one of the restaurant's favored dishes, a dense seafood gazpacho. A moist, pale-orange savarin might sit on one of the shelves, or perhaps a berry tart, or a macadamia nut or Linzer torte, these flanked by layer cakes of brown and white chocolate. Always, bowls of fresh fruit abound—grapes, pears, apples, peaches—a must for the Langs.

"We consider fruit extremely important in the Café," says George. "We even have an in-house fruit ripening program. At least half a dozen fresh fruits are always available, and fresh fruit sorbets are made twice every day."

Up a couple of steps from this long front room, through an area referred to as the mezzanine and around a bend to the right, is the Café des Artistes' small bar, a cul-de-sac called the Christy Room. The bar runs the length of the room, its end display a sculpted wire hard-boiled egg holder, a fixture of café restaurants in Europe. The bar is separated by an aisle from booths and small banquettes. Many regulars prefer to dine in this area's relative privacy, where even club soda is served in a champagne glass. At the far end of the bar nestle two round tables, almost hidden, where more publicly known patrons of the restaurant often choose to eat.

Another part of the restaurant that lends itself to privacy is the Parlor. Turn left rather than right as you enter the foyer of the Hotel des Artistes and you'll find yourself in this tiny extension of the Café. Once an office, it resembles a European coffeehouse in miniature, featuring an oak bar ornately embossed with zinc, which Jenifer found in Paris. Dark varnished walls, framed prints, and menu items written on the walls and mirrors in white scrolled calligraphy ("George's handwriting," says Jenifer) contribute to the ambience.

A few bentwood stools are at the bar, and the small café tables, their tops marquetry inlays of chessboards,

A highly polished baker's table is the centerpiece of the main dining room.

A Garden Oasis

Against the leaded windows of the Café des Artistes, a thicket of potted plants lines the shelves behind the main dining room's long, deep-green banquette. Interspersed with copper kettles, a duck press, small warming tables, and ceramic vases, the greenery offers a lush mirror of nearby Central Park.

"The Langs say it should be like a garden, a northeastern garden," says their floral designer of more than a decade, Dennis Cremmins. "They feel people should be stepping from New York into a greenhouse like you might have in your home." Begonias and azaleas sit among feathery ferns, red-splotched caladium, palms, and rhododendrons. Sage and asparagus ferns sprout from other pots. At Easter there are white lilies, at Christmas red poinsettias. Luncheon customers delight in this room, for on a bright day, usually around two o'clock, the sun floods and flickers through the collected greenery. At night the plantings are illuminated dramatically by tiny ceiling spotlights, creating a warm and wonderful copse in which diners can forget about the city outside.

The Café's greenhouse-like setting offers a lush mirror of nearby Central Park.

will accommodate no more than a dozen people. At the entry to the bar is another traditional coffeehouse touch, wood racks holding newspapers.

The Parlor is open evenings for dinner, for pastries and sweets, or as a private room for those who might like the idea of dining in what could be a coffeehouse-restaurant in Europe. Vienna? Perhaps. Paris? Perhaps. "I wanted this to feel like a comfortable little neighborhood place in Paris," Jenifer says. "Or Budapest," says George, with a bow to his native Hungary. European, to be sure, but more importantly, Jenifer says, "to continue the look of the Café des Artistes that George designed years ago."

George takes particular pride in the fact that he has never advertised his restaurant. "Word of mouth is our advertising," he says. Similarly, he notes, "The Café is never mentioned in wine magazines or by wine writers, nor is it included in wine festivals" by those he calls "winecompoops." The favored wine service is a basket of four reds or whites, all of a family, from France, Germany, Italy, and California. Lang has also added wines from the vineyard he owns and operates in Hungary. All are offered at the same price, $22 a bottle. The guests choose from the basket. "They feel as if they have discovered something," says Lang, "and in truth, they have."

A more traditional wine list appears on the daily menu as "Celebration Wines." Champagne is served by the carafe, which, Lang says, "fits my concept of reverse chic quite neatly."

It is also in keeping with the steadfast belief that the Café des Artistes ought never, on any level—surroundings, service, food, or drink—be regarded by its patrons as intimidating. In the beginning, George says, "I thought of the Café as a warm, pleasant restaurant for the neighbors. It has evolved into that, although happily not just for the neighbors on West 67th Street but for neighbors around the globe."

It has indeed.

Customer care at the Café dictates that all bar patrons are served drinks within one minute of ordering.

Café des Artistes

CHAPTER TWO

THE MAESTRO, THE DIRECTOR, AND THE CHEF

I t would not be inappropriate to suggest that the Café des Artistes is perhaps the defining achievement of George Lang's long career as a restaurant developer, food consultant, culinary historian and essayist, and all-purpose gastronomic guru. This, though his career is spiked with numerous noteworthy achievements: He once flew to London with cargo jets full of provisions from 26 of the 50 states for a Jeffersonian dinner he orchestrated at the Savoy.

Over the years, Lang's fanciful imagination, the enormous breadth of his knowledge about food, and an apparent bottomless well of creative juices have contributed to the development of more than 300 restaurants and projects throughout the world. This, appropriately, by a fellow who has been called by *Fortune* magazine "the man who invents restaurants." But all of these efforts were for employers or clients. The Café is the first restaurant Lang has ever owned, the one he shepherds most carefully and picks over constantly.

He is not a man wedded to modesty. "I basically invented the concept of international restaurant consulting," Lang once told an interviewer. The subtitle of his memoir, *Nobody Knows the Truffles I've Seen*, published in 1997, reads bluntly, "Restaurateur-Raconteur Extraordinaire."

Lang once confided to a newspaper writer that a friend described his mind as "a magic faucet from which the ideas would pour the minute I turn it on." It is a description in which he revels, one he believes to be accurate. His book *The Cuisine of Hungary*, an exhaustive study of the regional foods and recipes of his native country, remains in print almost 30 years after it was published.

Similarly, it would be inadequate to describe his wife, Jenifer, as the Café des Artistes' managing director. That is her working title, but she brings to their professional partnership her background as a food scholar and editor of the American edition of *Larousse Gastronomique*, the massive French encyclopedia of all things culinary.

Her mission at the Café is to ensure that the restaurant's philosophy—"George's vision," she calls it—is maintained. "We have always insisted that it not be intimidating, and that is something I have worked at, and do every day," she says.

The third member of the triumvirate that sees to the continuity of the Café des Artistes is its chef, Thomas Ferlesch, an accomplished cook with experience in Europe, Asia, and the Americas. Though some might disagree with the humility of the Vienna-born Ferlesch's self-assessment, he maintains that, "I am not an artist. I am a craftsman." He adds, however, that "to include artistry, you must be a craftsman first."

Artist or craftsman, there is no doubt that he is a superb cook. He hews to the Lang philosophy that diners who come to the Café des Artistes should be treated "as if they were walking into somebody else's dining room, that of a friend." Of his cooking, Ferlesch says, "I believe in real food, what people cook at home." He came to the Café des Artistes after writing a letter to Lang. "Mr. Lang knew my food, bourgeois food, country-style food," he recalls.

This background, combined with a fascination with improving and expanding it, makes Ferlesch the ideal

Jenifer Lang offers opinions on chef Ferlesch's creations.

"By and large, chefs do not taste. They depend upon routine. I say routine is the cancer of restaurants. If we do not taste, we lose consistency." —*George Lang*

A Rough Road to Restaurant Success

George Lang was born György Deutsch in 1924 in Székesfehérvár, Hungary, 35 miles from Budapest. His father, Simon, a tailor, and his mother, Ilona, were a cultured couple, and György was brought up with a love of music and a certain skill with the violin. Like other Jewish families in Hungary, the Deutsches became victims of Nazi anti-Semitism. Young György was sent to a labor camp when he was 20, his parents to Auschwitz, where they would die. He escaped from the labor camp and traveled from place to place in Hungary. Initially eluding the Arrow Cross, a pro-Nazi Hungarian political militia, he managed later to use this group as a temporary cover by joining under an assumed name. Eventually, however, he was discovered and, as he recounts it, the night before he was to be executed, Russian troops liberated Budapest.

György, though, was not freed. Identified as a member of the Arrow Cross, he was imprisoned for seven months, then tried for war crimes. Although he was acquitted, he decided that the Hungary of 1946 was no longer his country. With his cousin Eva and her husband and his cherished violin, György escaped, making his way as a refugee to the United States.

On his way to the top, George Lang worked as everything from a tailor to an encyclopedia salesman.

Because his family name, Deutsch, translated as "German," he discarded it and took his mother's maiden name, arriving in America as George Lang.

He was a janitor, a garment worker, a tailor, and a door-to-door encyclopedia salesman, all the while continuing his violin studies. His hard work paid off when Lang played a season with the Dallas Symphony. But while he was able to perform the Mendelssohn concerto on a very high level, when he heard Jasha Heifetz play that piece one night in Lewisohn Stadium, Lang realized that he would never be able to play like his idol. "I went home, looked at my violin with affection, put it back in its case, and slid it under the bed," Lang recalls. "The next morning, I went to look for a job."

He became a busboy at Reubens, then zigzagged through a series of jobs as saucier, captain, waiter, and headwaiter, leaving each as he squeezed a drop of learning from it.

He was assistant banquet manager at the Waldorf-Astoria under the legendary host and party-giver Claude Philippe, and later a senior vice president of the Brass Rail, for a time one of the country's more forward-looking food organizations. That led to the position of corporate vice president for the original Restaurant Associates, acknowledged to have been a revolutionary force in food service not only in the United States but abroad. Its continuing shrine is the Four Seasons, which Lang managed for two years.

chef for the Café des Artistes. "By and large, chefs do not taste," Lang says. "They depend upon routine. I say routine is the cancer of restaurants. If we do not taste, we lose consistency." Ferlesch, he says, "has unending, unstoppable enthusiasm," and Lang calls him the ultimate craftsman.

The admiration is mutual. "It is interesting to work with Mr. Lang," Ferlesch says. "He has incredible knowledge. I can learn from him on all different levels."

Learning and working together are the cornerstones of the kitchen's philosophy. "A good marriage is based upon a lot of things, including being good partners, and other aspects apart from sentiment," Lang explains. "The best chefs have to be partners with their restaurateurs. At the Café we are different; we are a ménage à trois, inspiring, checking, criticizing, and praising each other."

Ferlesch works well in that environment. "The open chef is the most desirable. One who is willing to consider," Lang says. "Some chefs need guidelines and borders, and welcome input. Others will recoil, crawl into their shells, so strictness will be counterproductive."

Jenifer adds, "When we offer ideas, we want Thomas to say yes or no. In many ways he gives our menu his imprimatur. But we all understand that the dishes must fit into a niche in our menu. While the last word is George's or mine, if Thomas said no, an emphatic no, to a dish, it would not go on the menu."

While Lang appreciates the give and take of the Café's triumvirate, he is also an entrepreneur who is most comfortable running his own show. He opened his personal consulting firm in 1969. Over the years he has developed restaurants and food complexes, great and small, for hotel chains and cruise lines,

Chef Thomas Ferlesch hews to the Lang credo that diners should be treated "as if they were walking into somebody else's dining room, that of a friend."

for shahs and kings and presidents, for countries in Europe, the Middle East, Latin America, and Asia.

In 1990, he returned to his native Hungary to restore and energize Gundel, the most famous restaurant in Budapest, a grand-luxe establishment opened in 1894. Lang owns Gundel in partnership with Ronald Lauder, the diplomat and international businessman who is the son of Estée Lauder, founder of the cosmetics empire. Just a few steps from Gundel, Lang opened the Owl's Castle, a rustic restaurant with a female chef, female cooks, female management, and a female staff that serves only traditional Hungarian home cooking.

Lang regularly commutes to Budapest to see to Gundel and the Owl's Castle, but he always returns to the Café des Artistes. When he is not at the Café, prowling about, fussing over the *cochonnaille* (charcuterie) and head cheeses, sticking a finger into the *brandade* (a purée of salt cod, olive oil, and milk) to test its texture, opening wine bottles at random to check for corkiness, Jenifer is keeping a sharp eye on all.

Is the butter pressed perfectly into its ramekin? Is the bread cut into those particular thick lengths and wedged upright into its cane basket? Does the lentil soup contain sufficient bits of smoked ham? Let it not be thought that Jenifer is merely a periodic substitute for her husband. In a small book of recipes of Café des Artistes dishes, published in.1984, George praises Jenifer for her "inspiration and virtuoso skill in the kitchen" in not only preserving the restaurant's traditional recipes but giving them freshness and currency.

Jenifer, a graduate of the Culinary Institute of America and for some time a working cook, is the author of *Tastings: The Best from Ketchup to Caviar*, a thoughtful look at the essential tastes of many common foods. She has also written *Jenifer Lang Cooks for Kids*, a collection of recipes simple enough for even the most impatient. She has written for *The New York Times*, *Elle*, and *McCall's*, had a column in *The Washington Post*, and demonstrated her cookery skills on such network TV programs

No mere substitute for George, Jenifer Lang brings a wide range of culinary knowledge to the table.

(Almost) Never
Say No

Although the Café's doctrine, preached by managing director Jenifer Lang, is "We never, never say no," there is an exception that proves the rule.

One evening, in her occasional capacity as "engagement counselor," Lang says she arranged for a "lovely table, to be followed by a limousine that would arrive precisely after dessert, when this gentleman would propose to his lady friend. It was all prepared. The dinner was perfect, as was the dessert. Then he produced the ring and proposed. She said no and walked out. The poor fellow sat there for a bit then looked up at our waitress. 'Do you want to marry me?' he asked. She too said no. So, you see, we do say no sometimes."

It was suggested that had George Lang been hovering over the table that night, he might have instructed the waitress to say, "Yes, but I'm afraid this evening I cannot."

as *Good Morning America* and *The Today Show.* George is quick to point out her managerial instincts, as well.

The staff supports a nonstop kitchen where Ferlesch reigns over a menu that changes by a third every day, its composition determined by market availability. He delights in introducing unusual items. "One day I just felt like making some tripe," he says. "I know it's not a dish that's going to make people form a line around the block, but people ordered it, and that made me feel good. They have confidence in our kitchen."

His tenure as executive chef at the Café des Artistes is for him the pinnacle of a personal adventure. He began his career as a kitchen apprentice at the age of 14 in Vienna, where he attended the Gastgewerbefachschule, a hotel school of great prestige.

"I loved to eat," he says, "and I always liked the aspect of my profession that allowed me to work and travel the world at the same time." For three years after his graduation, he worked in Switzerland, but his desire to use his skills as an excuse to travel took him to restaurants on the Côte d'Azur, in Morocco and Italy, and then to Austria. While in Austria he cooked in a monastery, where for a feast of St. Martin he stayed up all night to prepare 350 geese because there were only four ovens.

He scooted over to Bermuda for a while, then heard that a Viennese restaurant, Vienna 79, was being planned in Manhattan. He flew to New York and was hired as sous-chef. The restaurant, initially awarded three stars, gained a fourth a year later when Ferlesch took over as chef. That made Ferlesch, at 23, the youngest chef ever to have received that honor, the highest of restaurant ratings. He subsequently opened Jean Lafitte, in its day one of New York's best bistros, and managed Chapiteau and Café Un Deux Trois. At his wife's urging, he wrote to Lang, and in 1991 he accepted the position of executive chef.

For George and Jenifer Lang and for Thomas Ferlesch, the watchwords of the Café des Artistes are accommodation with style. To which George adds an aphorism gleaned from the pronouncements of Queen Victoria, "Things taste better in small places."

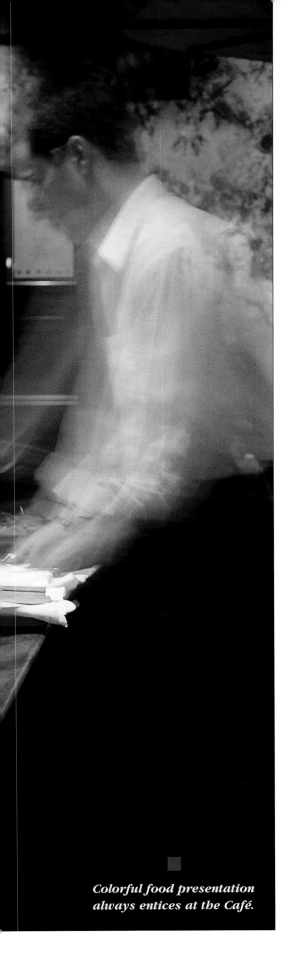

Colorful food presentation always entices at the Café.

Nudes frolic with gleeful abandon in this detail from Spring.

Café des Artistes

CHAPTER THREE

THOSE MURALS, SO NAUGHTY, SO NICE

The lovely round young women who enliven the walls of the Café des Artistes have been described variously as nubile, lush, romantic, sensual, chaste, sylphlike, pert, seductive, innocent, and wanton. With nary an attempt to hide their naked bodies, the figures gambol, skylark, caper, frolic, and leap about—through shrubs and foliage, among flowers, swinging from vines, wading around lily pads, and bathing with swans in gleeful abandon. These voluptuous murals have been a star attraction at the Café des Artistes for decades.

The women disporting themselves so joyfully in these murals set the tone for the Café des Artistes today quite as they were meant to when Howard Chandler Christy painted the first group in 1934 (he completed the sister paintings in 1942). They connoted then, and make us consider now, the upscale bohemianism of West 67th Street during that era, inviting unabashed viewing. It is not at all an exaggeration to suggest that one's grilled Portobello mushrooms or confit of duck simply taste better in their presence.

All 36 women, skin tones restored to a bright and shimmering rosiness, the boskiness surrounding them glowing in yellows and emeralds, are the work of one of the most commercially successful artists of the early twentieth century. A sought-after portrait painter, occasional muralist, and illustrator of books and patriotic posters, Christy created *The Christy Girl*, a somewhat more saucy and suggestive counterpart to *The Gibson Girl* of his contemporary, Charles Dana Gibson.

Christy was the first tenant to buy an apartment (duplex studio suite number 707) in the Hotel des Artistes when the building opened in 1917. As such, he was surely one of the first to regard the Café des Artistes as a club. He ate and drank there on a regular basis, and it has been suggested that his excessive Café bills led to the murals. Whether that was the case or not, he painted the murals without a fee, in return for an agreement that he would never again have to pay a bill at the Café des Artistes.

Initially, the plan for decorating the Café was for several of the artists on the block to each paint a mural for one of its walls, in an effort to bring excitement, and new business, to the Café in its post–Great Depression days. That idea foundered in squabbling over placement, subject matter, status, and fees. Christy stepped in with his proposal and it was snapped up. Upon completion, murals covered most of the wall space, on canvases fastened to the walls.

The paintings leave no doubt as to Christy's admiration for the female form. All of the women are egregiously nude, flaunting themselves mischievously, yet simultaneously chaste. A blonde nude in *The Swing Girl* pushes an auburn-haired nude through the air as she hangs on to a suspended vine, while two other women dance among bowers of flowers. In *Parrot Girl*, a wide-eyed and smiling woman shares her forest branch with a huge, plumed bright red parrot. Seven women play in the waters of *The Fountain of Youth*, a winged god Pan standing atop the back of one of them as she lies on a rock; and in the vast *Spring*, which covers the entire rear wall of the Café,

The murals lend warmth and romance to the Café dining experience.

It has been suggested that Howard Chandler Christy's excessive Café bills led to the murals, which he painted free of charge.

women rest, sprawl, dance, chat, read, and generally enjoy each other's presence against a backdrop of budding trees and flowering shrubbery.

The bright and urgent women of *Fall* sit among foliage and shrubs as they look down on the restaurant's sought-after Table Two, just inside the entrance. Off to the right is one of the two male figures to appear in the murals, a loin-clothed fellow who smiles winningly at his nude female companion. Some call the mural "Tarzan," others, "The Buster Crabbe Scene," for one of the actors who portrayed the ape man in Hollywood. No less an expert than John Canaday, the former art critic for *The New York Times*, described this bare-chested fellow as a "single young male, by the way just as pink as the girls and grinning like

■

The bright and urgent women of **Fall** *peer down on the sought-after Table Two.*

A Mural's Inspiration

A number of women modeled for Howard Chandler Christy, all of whom, it is said, developed a fondness for him. One, Olga Steckler, told an interviewer years ago that Christy was "plump and warm and lovely," perhaps quite like herself in one of the murals. She, like Christy and others of the easel set, was enamored of the Café des Artistes. "In the thirties and forties, a lot of artists and models lived in Des Artistes and we all ate at the Café," she told the interviewer. "It was the most fabulous place to be. It was our restaurant." Another of Christy's models was Nancy May Palmer, who posed for his World War II posters and later became his second wife.

There were always rumors about who had posed for Christy's Café murals. A restorer who worked on them said Palmer had been the model for all of them. Lending credence to that claim is a tale told by denizens of West 67th Street. Though the paintings were restored occasionally, some say that Palmer, year after year, would show up at the Café des Artistes with bars of facial soap, warm water, and rolls of gauze to gently wash down the murals. One suggestion was that she was symbolically giving herself a bath.

Perhaps there were several models. Steckler said that she had posed, as had two sisters named Ford, one of whom, she claimed, had a daughter by Christy. In fact, many women would hint that they had been models for Christy's nudes.

This sort of speculation doesn't bring a twinkle to everyone's eye. As George Lang recalls, at dinner one evening, "A couple was getting ready to leave. It was an odd time, about seven o'clock, and they were obviously upset. When I got to the desk the man was saying, 'We've got to leave. We've got to leave.' I gave him my card and asked if anything was wrong with our food or the service. He said that was not the problem.

"They had been sitting in the front room, at a table facing the *Spring* mural. He said to me, 'Suddenly I remembered that my mother, at a birthday party where she had had a bit to drink, told us that as a young woman she had modeled for Howard Chandler Christy. I was looking at the wall, and I thought of my mother, without clothes, among all those diners, and I could not finish my dinner. I am so sorry.' " Lang promised the man that on his next visit, he would be seated in the mural-free back room, which was the case when the man returned a few months later.

Parrot Girl *shares her forest branch with a huge plumed bird.*

All of the women are egregiously nude, flaunting themselves mischievously, yet simultaneously chaste.

mad, [who] seems to be serving as a kind of scoutmaster for the picnic. We have not yet quite figured out the iconography."

Just around the corner is the other male, an armored *Ponce de Leon* enjoying the nude women dancing in the pools and flowers around him.

Although the murals have been the core of the restaurant's setting for years, they were almost lost to the Café's diners. When George Lang signed a lease with the cooperative to take over the restaurant in 1975, a dispute erupted over who owned them. Romeo Sterlini, who was at the time sole owner of the Café, argued that the Christy murals were his.

Lang recalls that the local papers had a field day with the ensuing battle, with headlines blaring "Café des Artistes Packing Its Paintings to Leave Co-Op" and "Landmark Will Be Closing. The Café des Artistes at 1 West 67th Street is shutting its doors for the last time on May 31st."

Lang says it was important to him to keep the murals, because he believed customers would greatly enjoy "basking in Howard Chandler Christy's sun and the flesh colors of the flirtatious ladies. The murals please everyone, regardless of the level of art appreciation, regardless of age. They are a wonderful, direct link to the building's past, and a bit of titillation."

One afternoon, Lang was sitting at the bar and Sterlini, in passing, pointed to a spot across from the bar. As Lang recalls, Sterlini said, "There used to be a small Christy painting there years ago, but a guest fell in love with it and we sold it to him."

That line triggered an idea that turned out to be the solution, Lang says. "That second, it occurred to me that if no one had noticed the painting was missing, perhaps the four framed Christy girls that were removable and not part of the murals could be offered to Sterlini in exchange for his leaving the Café within 24 hours, especially if we sweetened the deal with a few hundred thousand dollars.

A detail from **Spring***, which covers the Café's rear wall.*

PORTRAIT OF AN ARTIST

Howard Chandler Christy and his career were microcosms of his time. A talented country fellow from Morgan County, Ohio, Christy gravitated to the gaminess of New York, submerged himself in it, and made it his own. Born in 1873, he sold his first drawings at the age of 13 to the *Toledo Blade*. He visited New York City on and off from the ages of 17 to 20 to study at the Art Students League, the National Academy of Design, and Cooper Union.

He began illustrating books and magazines in his early twenties, and in 1898, during the Spanish American War, worked as an artist and correspondent for *Leslie's Weekly* . His war drawings also appeared in *Scribner's, Harpers,* and *Century* magazines.

In 1906, he published his first book about "The Christy Girl," titled *The American Girl*. It was an immediate success, as popular as Charles Dana Gibson's girls. By the time he moved into a grand studio at the Hotel des Artistes, much of his work, along with that of Gibson and James Montgomery Flagg (creator of the "I Want You" Uncle Sam poster), was for the war effort. The poster for which Christy is perhaps most famous? A smiling woman, her eyes seductively half-closed, wearing a sailor's hat and uniform, her torso thrust forward, saying, "Gee! I Wish I Were a Man. I'd Join the Navy." Franklin Delano Roosevelt, Secretary of the Navy at the time, said that the poster was responsible for recruiting thousands of men.

Following the war, Christy painted portraits of famous people, including William Randolph Hearst, Lillian Russell, General John J. Pershing, President Warren G. Harding, President and Mrs. Calvin Coolidge, Will Hays, the notorious Hollywood film censor, and Charles Evans Hughes. Christy's travels to Europe brought him commissions to paint Queen Marie of Romania, Prince Phillip of Hesse, and Benito Mussolini.

In the late twenties and early thirties, Christy was depressed and exhausted by his travels and the demands of his portrait work. Confiding to friends that he thought he might be going blind, he went quietly to the country to work. There, he began to paint bucolic landscapes as well as nudes, producing in 1929 a huge canvas entitled *Two Nudes*. It features a pair of women remarkably like those who would later adorn the Café's walls, one standing and looking back over her shoulder, the other stretched back toward the viewer.

The next year, he created somewhat of a sensation with two five-paneled screens, each entitled, *Damsels in a Forest with Knight*. On each, female nudes, in forest and pool, danced among flowers and branches, in and out of ponds, in a variety of erotic poses. They are virtually identical to those he was to paint later at the Café.

In this period he also painted more portraits, of Will Rogers, Amelia Earhart, and several of his West 67th Street neighbors, such as William Beebe, Richard Barthelmess, Lawrence Tibbett, and Jo Davidson, as well as a series of the World War I ace Captain Eddie Rickenbacker. He continued to paint and sketch in his Hotel des Artistes studio until his death on March 3, 1952.

"The next morning, his attorney called mine and we took possession of the restaurant, alas without the *Swan Girl* and several of her sisters." The agreement was also trumpeted in the local press: "The Nudes Will Stay on Café's Walls." *Swan Girl*, depicting a nude, perhaps an innocent Leda, wading between two swans, can be enjoyed now as the frontispiece of a small commemorative booklet printed by the Café.

Lang tells a story "that might be true" about the murals. "Sometime between 1932 and 1934, some say that Marcel Duchamp asked a janitor to let him into the Café des Artistes after hours. It was rumored on West 67th

The murals leave no doubt as to Howard Chandler Christy's admiration for the female form.

"The murals please everyone, regardless of the level of art appreciation, regardless of age. They are a wonderful, direct link to the building's past, and a bit of titillation." —*George Lang*

Street that Duchamp painted part of a figure. Did he? Or a face. Did he? This was reported to Christy, who thought a bit and said, 'That's okay.' " So there may even be a bit of Duchamp among the nudes, a thought that pleases the block.

Christy is remembered not only for his art but for his personality. Norman Rockwell, his one-time neighbor, described him sitting at the Café des Artistes bar, "short, stocky, pugnacious Christy, boomingly cheerful," and said of him, "Publicity and he were right for each other, like pearls and duchesses or cole slaw and church suppers."

The rear room that houses the Café's bar is known as the Christy Room. It features some Christy drawings kept by his widow until her death and bought at an auction of the estate. Of particular interest is a drawing of the operatic diva and movie star Grace Moore, signed, "To Grace Moore With Admiration, Howard Chandler Christy." Just under this inscription is another which reads, "To Howard Chandler Christy from Grace Moore, Also With Admiration." It arouses occasional tongue clucking on the block.

Christy himself appears on the walls as well. A portrait of the artist done by his friend and colleague James Montgomery Flagg oversees the bar.

In evaluating the Christy nudes, the illustrator and satirist Edward Sorel said, "We're not responding to great art; we're responding to the time when it was done. It's art that we love to love. He must have believed in what he was doing, because there's a lot of tender, loving care there, a lot of energy, like Rubens. They're very desirable."

Perhaps the late Brendan Gill, a passionate critic, said it best: "The nudes have been described as reflecting 'the artist's splendid sense of design, and the use of color and form,' and that may well be the case; what matters more to us is that they do honor to his randy old evergreen heart. The Café is a happier place for the relish with which he carried out the commission of the board of directors." Just so.

Many old-timers say this loin-clothed fellow, one of only two men in the paintings, is modeled after Buster Crabbe.

Café des Artistes

CHAPTER FOUR

THE CAFÉ REBORN

Removing the grime of time and restoring light to Howard Chandler Christy's rosy murals was not the only task George Lang set for himself when he took over the Café des Artistes in 1975, but it was surely the most visible. When he assumed control, the restaurant had "a certain seedy charm, if you call grimy paintings, filthy red carpets, and surly waiters in a pseudo-Gothic yellow-and-black room charming," he says. "The Café's curtains carefully closed in the outside world and closed out the inside world, whichever."

His comments on its food are just as withering. "The menu was stereotyped and tried to be everything to everybody at all times, ranging from shrimp cocktail to smoked salmon, fillet of sole amandine to roast beef and chocolate mousse, not forgetting the bought pastries and the ever-present pear poached in red wine." He asserts that in some restaurants that dessert is nothing more than a canned pear with "collected leftover red wine poured over it."

But Lang enjoys a challenge. He has suggested that "being a restaurateur who takes over an ailing, comatose, virtually dead restaurant on the West Side of New York is like being a purser on the *Titanic*."

He welcomed the opportunity, in part, he says, because of an afternoon almost 30 years earlier. In

*The **Spring** mural was moved, along with the dining room's rear wall, to create more kitchen space.*

1946, soon after his arrival in the United States as a young immigrant planning to become a violinist, he auditioned for music teacher Vera Fonaroff, "this tiny little lady in a duplex at the Hotel des Artistes. "After all the deaths and the labor camps, I was eyes and cheekbones, and she saw I was ready to eat something, or her, whatever was chewable. It was about three o'clock and I'd had no lunch, so she took me down to the Café des Artistes and I was dazzled! How it looked that day!"

In 1946 the Café des Artistes still glowed as the fashionable clubhouse of Christy and his fellow artists and performers along West 67th Street. The residents of the Hotel des Artistes patronized the restaurant so frequently that the kitchen staff, who collectively called themselves Common Chef, produced their own little book of cookery practices, entitled *Retiring the Tyrant Cookstove*, and urged tenants to order from them.

The Café was a neighborhood restaurant as well. During Prohibition, it became a tea room, though it is said on the block that very strong tea was available most evenings. The restaurant closed briefly after Prohibition, then reopened with an after-tea party to celebrate the repeal of the Volstead Act. New York Mayor Jimmy Walker and James Farley, the powerful Democratic politician who later became Postmaster General, were guests at that affair.

Post-Prohibition, the Café's proprietor was a former speakeasy owner, but in 1941 it was sold to Charles and Marie Turner. Turner and Romeo Sterlini subsequently became partners. Through the fifties and sixties, the Café des Artistes, referred to then as The Des, virtually became the official restaurant for

Strategically placed mirrors mask spots where murals were removed.

A Haven for Artists

It was called a hotel, but it never was. From the start, the Hotel des Artistes was a cooperative apartment building with squash courts and a pool. It even had a ballroom that, for a time, was rented to the American Broadcasting Company for live TV.

To maintain the facade of a hotel, tenant-owners installed a reception desk to answer telephone calls and take messages and mail. This also permitted the apartment to house a restaurant. The Café des Artistes was nominally a public restaurant in those early days, but it functioned more as an in-house commissary to the tenants of the studios above.

Many of those huge ateliers either had no kitchens at all or had tiny, barely adequate Pullman kitchenettes. Residents would shop or have food bought for them, and then deliver it to the restaurant's kitchen. There it would be prepared to specification and sent up to the apartments at prescribed times, via a system of electronically controlled dumbwaiters.

The grand scale of the hotel's apartments was noted by writer Fannie Hurst, who occupied a palatial triplex studio and apartment with 30-foot ceilings from 1932 until her death in 1968. Its very size and the Gothic woodwork in it forced her, she said, to shop for heavy, dark furniture that would be in keeping with the apartment.

The hotel's famous residents read like a who's who of the artistic community of the time. Rudolph Valentino, sculptors Jo Davidson and Augustus John, the great classical actress Alla Nazinmova, artists Norman Rockwell and Howard Chandler Christy, Lawrence Tibbett, the Metropolitan Opera baritone, and orchestra leader Paul Whiteman all took apartments there, and actress Mae Murry sublet her opulent flat to Noël Coward.

The hotel was also the birthplace of one of this country's most enduring traditions: the Miss America Pageant. Dreamed up by James Montgomery Flagg and Howard Chandler Christy for a masquerade party they called the Chu Chin Chow Ball, it started out less as a pageant than as a lark. Edith Hyde, the first Miss America, was chosen at that ball over a handful of Ziegfeld girls and a couple of young actresses, ingenues typical of those who, at the tiime, were just beginning to be called starlets. Hyde was given a gilded apple as the symbol of her reign on February 1, 1919. It did not matter to the partygoers that she was not at all a miss. She was married to a fellow named Robbins, and the mother of two children, but who cared? Certainly not the denizens of West 67th Street, who endeavored always to have good times, laced with frivolity.

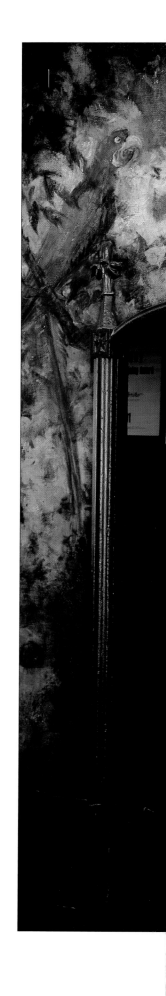

Servers going to and from the kitchen pass through the vast playground of Spring.

Mirrors in the Parlor are inscribed by George Lang, in the style of a European coffeehouse.

the American Broadcasting Company TV and radio crowd, whose offices were just one block away.

Though it continued to be a comfortable, familiar place for the artists and their neighbors during this period, it declined into a restaurant without luster, and ebbed financially as well. This combination of circumstances prompted the Hotel des Artistes cooperative to seek out George Lang, a longtime West 67th Street neighbor, to resuscitate the Café.

Faced with the shabby interior and some empty spaces formerly filled with Christy paintings that had gone with the former owner, Lang chose to exhibit works by customers who were amateur artists. He filled other spots with mirrors to reflect the murals that remained.

Lang closed the restaurant for a while to reconfigure it. The rear wall of the Café's main room was moved forward to create serving, preparation, and pantry space, and the *Spring* mural went with it. Its young women now occupy the entire wall, their vast playground interrupted only by an opening through which servers pass. In the front of the restaurant another mural, *Fall*, was moved to form the backdrop for the desirable Table Two, which is usually booked far in advance. That space had been a checkroom. Lang also tore out the dumbwaiter shaft.

These changes created the three rooms that now constitute the Café des Artistes. "I tried to preserve and restore the premises in such a manner that even old habitués would not recognize any change, even though what we did was a total restoration," Lang explains. "The block is still populated by a number of artists, ballet dancers, choreographers, photographers, portrait painters, and authors. Especially for this reason, I felt we should go back to the ancient Greek idea of a stoa, a place to gather and exchange ideas. I was resolved that the Café should be neither a gastronomic shrine nor a place for society to hang their 40-carat emeralds on. There are very few restaurants in New York that are contemporary to the Café des Artistes, and our aim has been the preservation of a New York landmark."

A street entrance to the restaurant was reopened. Carpets and lighting were installed. "I have a pathological concern with lighting. I have never met anyone, and that would include Catherine Deneuve, who does not look more beautiful with perfect lighting. No makeup is better than flattering lighting, which is still functional." Cove lighting along the tops of the murals now illuminates the paintings, and the heavy café curtains blocking the windows were replaced with boxed plants, permitting day and night to filter into the room. Lang purchased china by Schonwald and glassware by Zwiesel.

Many veteran members of the staff, from waiters and waitresses to cooks, barmen, and managers, were retained, as was former owner Charles Turner. Says Lang, "When I took over the restaurant, I felt that sense of continuity should apply to the staff. Charlie

In the early days, the Café kitchen functioned as an in-house commissary to the tenants of the Hotel des Artistes studios.

THAT CELEBRATED STREET

Perhaps no street in New York, that city of thousands of boulevards, avenues, blocks, lanes, alleys, and cul-de-sacs, has a past as richly textured as West 67th Street. It was once a street of bawds, a naughty block that was to become an artistic enclave packed with grand, multistoried apartments and studios decorated quite as the Elizabethans might have wished. Painters and sculptors, writers and musicians, actors and playwrights, were drawn to it.

That daring mistress of modern dance, Isadora Duncan, lived on the block, and so did Al Jolson. Noël Coward lived there for a time, as well, and much of Norman Rockwell's view of an innocent America was conceived by him in his studio on the block.

Rudolph Valentino resided on the street until the day he died. The day of his funeral is remembered for the sidewalk-to-sidewalk press of mourners who blocked West 67th Street to all traffic, including pedestrians. Twenty-eight separate, nonmatching shoes were found after the day's mourners were dispersed.

More recently, West 67th Street has been home to actor Carroll O'Connor, who created TV's Archie Bunker, and to the Public Broadcasting System anchorman Robert MacNeil. In an apartment on the street, Elizabeth and Lowell Hardwick conceived the estimable, and powerful, *New York Review of Books*. Its first issue was planned and dummied up following a Hardwick dinner party.

A significant time in the history of American art had its genesis on West 67th Street, and not only because such artists as Childe Hassam, Stuart Davis, and Gifford Beal lived and painted in their studios there. In their apartment at number 33, Walter and Louise Arensburg, art collectors and patrons, held convocations of what came to be called the Arensburg Circle. These evening salons, held at least three days each week, began after dinner and continued into the night.

Such artists as Marcel Duchamp, the revolutionary Cubist who startled the 1913 Armory Show with his *Nude Descending a Staircase*, would sit in the Arensburgs' apartment sharing talk, opinions, and prejudices with the likes of Joseph Stella, Charles Sheeler, Charles Demuth, Man Ray, and Francis Picabia. The poets and writers on the scene included William Carlos Williams, Wallace Stevens, Maxwell Bodenheim, and Carl Van Vechten. From those informal meetings sprang the notion of an art show to rival the Armory Show. In 1917, the group, calling themselves the Society of Independent Artists, held a vast show at the Grand Central Palace, open to all artists, no matter their fame or financial condition. Much of the work exhibited came from studios on the block.

Perhaps not coincidentally, the Arensburgs' apartment, scene of art and intellectual salons for almost 15 years, is now the home of Jenifer and George Lang and their children Simon and Gigi.

A detail from the lobby of the Hotel des Artistes (left), found on this storied street.

Once a street of bawds, West 67th Street became an artistic enclave packed with grand, multistoried apartments and studios decorated quite as the Elizabethans might have wished.

"I have a pathological concern with lighting. I have never met anyone, and that would include Catherine Deneuve, who does not look more beautiful with perfect lighting." —*George Lang*

had been the host of the Café for 34 years, so I valued his presence. He remained host for weekends and for brunch and stayed on for three years."

As the Café was being physically renovated and its staff reshaped, its philosophy of food changed as well. The new direction has enhanced the dining experience ever since the restaurant reopened on October 16, 1975. "The menu, I believed, should be neither aggressively one thing or another and should not be thought of as classic cuisine, haute cuisine, grande cuisine, bistro cuisine, *cuisine regionale*, any of those labels," says Lang. "At the same time, I knew we had to stay away from so-called Continental cuisine." He refuses to categorize the Café des Artistes' food, except to say that it is true to its roots of French bourgeois cooking.

As his menu was being shaped, Lang also knew what his reborn restaurant would not serve. "I eliminated the obviously symbolic dishes that stand for expensive restaurant elegance, such as crabmeat in everything and caviar. I eliminated all the clichéd French foods that are fashionable." This included quenelles, quiches, covering things with green peppercorns, and anything encased in pastry. "One day I am afraid a guest will find him or herself enveloped *en croûte*," Lang quips.

What emerged was a menu of style, tradition, and unarguable substance, with regular change instituted "in such a way that there will be no possibility of a stagnant menu. Salt is our enthusiasm," Lang says, "Pepper is our passion."

Bourride with Aïoli, a fish casserole is served Provencal-style.

Café des Artistes

CHAPTER FIVE

THE CAFÉ'S FOOD: TRADITION AS ART

Chef Thomas Ferlesch is in his kitchen, a few steps down from the dining area, dicing the meats that are the heart of Chef Thomas's Famous Country Pâté.

"I use only pork cheeks," he says, displaying scallops of meat, "and the jowl fat, because of its higher melting point. It is that fat accounts for those little pieces, the little white spots in the pâté." The chef's special blend is one-third pork cheeks, one-third jowl, and one-third chicken or duck livers, with garlic, rosemary, thyme, onions, and shallots marinated in port and cognac. He binds his pâté not with eggs but with bread. Coarsely broken walnuts and a little salt and pepper "fine tune" the pastiche that Ferlesch calls "a perfect mix."

As much as any preparation on its menu, this *pâté de campagne*, in place for years yet changed perceptibly by Ferlesch, illustrates what the Café's food is about: direct, intelligently seasoned cooking, without unnecessary embellishment; tradition wrought impeccably, yet with imagination and a fresh sense; tastes that have the capacity to evoke memories of meals past.

Consider Ferlesch's *brandade,* not exactly the classic from the Languedoc, where it is a smooth, pureed paste of mashed, salted cod, olive oil, and cream or milk, nor that of Provence, where garlic is added, but a version

The Langs invite the whole staff to get involved in selecting new dishes for the Café.

that combines both essential tastes. It is a dish dense with tradition, Ferlesch also adds pureed potatoes to the mixture, as is done widely in France.

Ferlesch's pot-au-feu is a grand boiled dinner with brisket of beef, chunks of vegetables, and marrow bones served in a rich bouillon created from seasoned chicken stock. This dish differs slightly from the versions of the Carcassone and Gascony but is quite close to that offered by the great French gastronome Maurice Edmond Sailland, known as Curnonsky, collector and interpreter of the French kitchen. It is a joyous dish that with each mouthful, including the scooped-out marrow, evokes the French countryside.

None of these preparations is a *soupcon-pour-soupcon* reproduction from Curnonsky or *Larousse Gastronomique*, or from French cooking giant Auguste Escoffier for that matter, but the roots are true. This is the food at Café des Artistes, dishes done right, always with some obeisance to tradition.

It was the kind of food that George Lang insisted upon when he took over the Café des Artistes. His vision has been executed well by Andre Guillou, who was chef at the Café for three decades, and by Ferlesch, his successor. "I once wrote that often, admiring a chef and getting to know him is like loving goose liver and then meeting the goose," Lang says. "Andre was an exception to this. He was classically trained and came from the same small Breton village that gave the cooking world so many sauciers."

Jenifer Lang took over as managing director in the same year that Ferlesch arrived to replace Guillou, who retired. She found the new young chef "so open to ideas that he was, and is, a joy to work with."

Creative changes abounded. On a menu where there had been marinated herring and shrimp cocktail, there now were gravlax marinated with dill and served with its skin crisp; salmon

The Café's superb cuisine, such as the Oxtail Stew, is always executed with some obeisance to tradition.

"I'm uneasy about such words as *create* and *invent*. When it comes to food, invention, and creation simply mean incomplete research." —*George Lang*

four ways, smoked, poached, tartar, and gravlax; and a seafood gazpacho that became one of the Café's signature dishes. *Pâté maison* gave way to the aforementioned thick, aromatic country pâté; to *rillettes*, that spreadable preparation from the Loire of pork shards cooked in their own fat, pounded and crocked; and to *cochonnailles*, which is an assortment including pâté, headcheese, prosciutto, and smoked pork loin served on a cutting board.

Chilled fruit cocktail and a green salad yielded to salads of distinction: arugula dressed with olive oil, lemon, and shavings of Parmigiano-Reggiano; endives with grapes, pears, roasted walnuts, and crumbled Stilton; and lentils and tomatoes accompanied by white anchovies. The Café also has its own rendition of the Waldorf salad, this with snow pea pods and walnuts, shaped like a small drum and ringed with thin scallops of fresh apple.

Many dishes have become standards over the years. George Lang calls these "our PSH, for Personalized Specialties of the House," preparations that he says have become identified with the Café. These include the seafood gazpacho, the pâté, and a black bean soup served in a porcelain pot with small dishes of tomatoes, chives, onions, and flat parsley around it.

Lang notes that he revived, among other traditional dishes, *oeufs Chimay,* a rich dish of simple ingredients. Hard-boiled eggs are halved, their yolks removed, and pounded to a paste with a duxelles of mushrooms, then returned, with a white béchamel sauce, Gruyere cheese, and a touch of butter laid over them before baking. "We had to test and retest it many times because the old recipes simply didn't work," he says.

Nor were smaller classics neglected. "I also brought back real mincemeat," says Lang, "which of course is made with various fruits, both candied and fresh, plus brandy, chopped

Attention to detail in the kitchen ensures that all dishes meet the Café's exacting standards.

The Café's food reflects direct, intelligently seasoned cooking, without unnecessary embellishment.

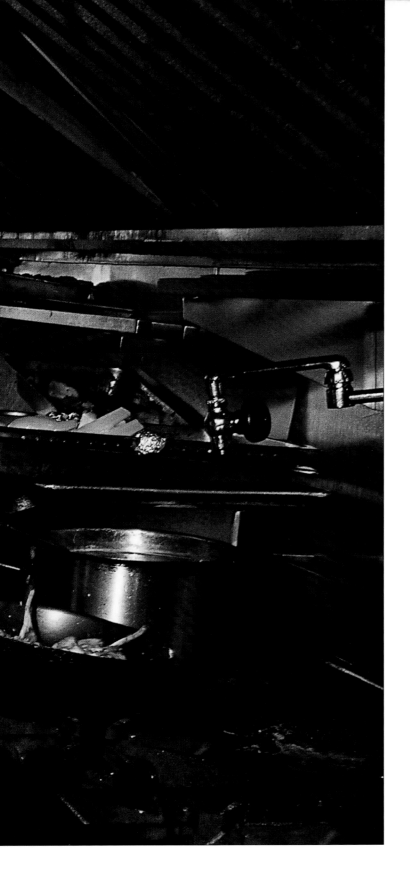

CREATIVE EXPERIMENTATION

*T*homas Ferlesch has proven to be the ideal chef for the Café des Artistes, not only for his skills, which are considerable, but for his openness and a restlessness that encourages change and experimentation.

"I always look to see if there is change possible," he says, citing his exquisite alteration of the Café's pâté. "But I will not change just to change, only to make it better. If I have no inspiration, I will not even try. I never fix a dish with a Band-Aid. I get to the bottom of it, I make a fix and let it stand."

George Lang cites an example of Ferlesch's creativity. "We are not a steak restaurant," he says. "For the first ten years, steak was not on our menu but was served on request. We are not a roast beef restaurant either. So how do you put beef on the menu? Thomas came up with the answer: Zwiebel Rostbraten, which is a thin steak, a braised paillard of rib eye that he serves with crisply fried onions and roasted potatoes. A Viennese dish from his early training, it was a brilliant solution, unheard of anywhere else in New York."

There is little mystery to the Café's menu; what distinguishes it is execution, and the intelligence the Langs and Thomas Ferlesch bring to the table.

beef, and beef suet. We serve it as an ice cream topping." The smaller things are important, and appreciated, he suggests, particularly when they might be unexpected. "Hardly anybody makes chutney well, yet it is one of the easiest things to do. In summertime, for instance, we serve a fresh peach chutney. In fall, we serve a fresh tomato chutney."

There is little mystery in the Café's menu; what distinguishes it is the execution, and the combined intelligence that the Langs and Ferlesch bring to the table. "I'm uneasy about such words as *create* and *invent*," says Lang. "When it comes to food, invention and creation simply mean incomplete research, because someone has already done it before. Our changes follow the seasons, which is a courtesy to our guests. When it is hot, we serve many cold dishes; when it is cold, we serve hot dishes."

Many of the dishes on the menu have come out of periodic staff tastings. Lang recalls a tasting some years ago where, "among other things, we tasted Wiener schnitzel sautéed in freshly rendered lard, lamb osso buco, mustard-roasted lamb, crisp boiled pigs' feet, and broiled white snapper steak, all of which eventually appeared on the menu with some modification. But there were also a lobster and crab cake, steak and sweetbreads on skewers, and a sweet potato salad, none of which will ever see our menu."

To top everything off, Lang swept the old dessert carte clean and, in an inspired moment, asked his West 67th Street neighbors to bake his desserts. When the word went out, more than 50 people paraded in with their sweets. "We would suspend meetings, set up plates and forks, and we would all become tasters and experts," Lang recalls. "What came in was unbelievably good and unbelievably bad, but we tasted them all." Eventually, the Café settled into a pattern where more than two dozen people made

■

Assembly of some Café specialties occurs at the baker's table.

ASPARAGUS-MANIA

When asparagus is in season, the Café always features an asparagus menu, which for George Lang is somewhat of a sentimental culinary journey. For many years during his career as a food consultant, a drawing of a bundle of asparagus spears was his company logo.

The produce-inspired design came about when he sat down with his friend, the graphic artist Milton Glaser, to think about corporate identity. "It should be something you love," Glaser said. "What do you love?"

Lang remembers replying, "Asparagus," and thus a familiar symbol was born, each of the spears in the bundle "one aspect of my large collection of work and interests."

His new corporation, Lang's Phase II, is represented by an asparagus fern logo, and his love of asparagus remains. Every spring brings a nightly asparagus menu, appropriately entitled, "Asparagus-mania."

One may order green asparagus from Salinas, California, either by the half dozen or the dozen, served with vinaigrette, drawn butter, hollandaise, Parmesan cheese, or topped with a fried egg. These might be followed with a bowl of chilled asparagus-yogurt soup, or thick spears crisped in beer batter and served with a dill and crème fraîche dip.

A preference might be for asparagus spears wrapped in gravlax or smoked salmon, or in prosciutto or pork loin. Or perhaps an asparagus risotto with either Black Forest ham or smoked salmon. Asparagus for lunch? There is a sandwich of rye bread topped with asparagus spears, Black Forest ham, and fontina cheese, then grilled. Any asparagus-lover's craving should be sated by that tour de force.

*Everyone, right down to the waitstaff, works to ensure
perfect presentation.*

Diners need a marrow spoon to savor every last drop of the Café's classic pot-au-feu, a grand boiled dinner.

their own specialties or sweets according to the Café's specifications. Lang says the selection ranged from "simple early-nineteenth-century recipes like rye bread torte and buttermilk pie to a complex dessert from my mother's kitchen, our Ilona Torte. I also recall well a pumpkin ice cream with pumpkin compote."

The Café des Artistes' neighbors are no longer its pastry kitchen. Because the city of New York requires that baking for hire must come from commercial, inspected kitchens, the practice was abandoned. The restaurant now makes some of its desserts and has small bakeries supply others to taste. The original Ilona Torte appears on the menu every day, other regular tenants are the Linzer torte, a Key lime pie that Lang considers a true "PSH," orange savarin served as toasted slices, and variations on crème brûlée.

In a section of the menu called "Only at the Café des Artistes" are the sweets made in the kitchen that day. These might include Ferlesch's bright take on traditional shortcake, a square of perfect shortbread with fresh stewed blueberries and blueberry sorbet; or an assortment put together into "The Great Dessert Plate;" or the "Chocolatissimo for Two," samples from as many as six chocolate desserts.

Nor should diners ignore "Mr. Christy's Ice Cream Palette," an assortment of ice creams arranged on a palette-shaped dish, these to be best enjoyed as one sits among Christy's playful young ladies.

Manager Susan Readwin, chef Thomas Ferlesch, and manager Ryan Buttner with the Café's staff.

Café des Artistes

CHAPTER SIX

THOSE WHO WAIT, AND SERVE

Hiran Pagan knows no other job, nor does he wish to. "Mr. Lang is not here all the time. He must be away sometimes to Budapest. But I am here. I worry about the Café des Artistes as much as he does," says Pagan. "Maybe more, but that makes me happy."

Pagan is a waiter at the Café, and has been for 46 years, as much a permanent fixture as any of those Christy murals. There can be no better illustration of the restaurant's concept of unbroken continuity than Hiram, who says of his job, "This is my life."

When Lang took over the Café, he found not only a tired and dreary restaurant but a waitstaff that "under the previous ownership was less than mediocre." Rather than dismiss all of them out-right and build an entirely new staff, Lang says he fell back upon his guiding philosophy of "subtle continuity."

He kept more than half of the staff for two good reasons, he says. "First because so many of them were well known and well liked by the customers; second, because I was struck immediately by their common enthusiasm about the impending changes and their willingness to adapt to what I wanted to do with the Café."

Those who remained became the core of a loyal and stable staff, a circumstance uncommon in the restaurant business in the United States, where every other wait person seems to be a musician, a dancer, or an actor waiting on tables simply to pay the rent. Many waiters at the Café des Artistes regard their jobs as permanent callings, a condition more common in Europe. In addition, many of those early waiters eventually became managers, products of the Langs' system of gradual progression and promotion from within.

Seeking talent outside is rare, and this policy has helped create an aura of family among the staff, a feeling that they are heirs to a tradition. Seldom are there "new" waiters at the restaurant; the majority have worked there for 10, 15, even 25 years. Janos Siess, a waiter and later a manager, began working at the Café in 1972, three years before the advent of George Lang. He stayed for 27 years, until his retirement, and says with a palpable wistfulness, "I might come back, I miss it so much."

In fact, Siess continued to work intermittently after his retirement. "I could not bear to leave it. I love the beauty, the setting, and always the intellectual people." Perhaps his favorite customer was the late Harry Reasoner, the TV newsman. "He was so casual, never pretentious," says Siess.

Despite his retirement, Siess keeps in touch with his co-workers. "We were always a family. We still

Hiran Pagan has worked at the Café since 1954.

"I served President Clinton when he came here. I asked him what he'd like to eat and he said, 'Whatever you eat.'" —*Hiran Pagan, waiter*

CUSTOMER CARE

When he took over the Café, George Lang reasoned that what the staff lacked was a philosophy encompassing behavior, appearance, and interaction with guests. So he compiled a manual for all employees, a strict compendium that specifies cleanliness, attire, and the welcoming nature of the restaurant he wanted the Café des Artistes to become.

The *Old Testament* of the Lang *Bible* is a changing document, a "logical, sensible system," according to Lang, that charges an employee with learning the name and composition of every dish on that day's menu, how each should be served, what wines to propose, and how the staff should anticipate guests' questions.

The *New Testament* is a printed manual of behavior, 62 pages long, that each employee must study and practice. The work of George and Jenifer Lang, it includes cookery terms and definitions, service practices particular to the Café des Artistes, basic dress, and comportment.

The *Bible* describes which entrances and exits waiters must use and how each table must be set up. It advises the staff to "always seat the guest," and cautions against "needless discussion among staff while on the floor." Addressing another critical area, the volume specifies that all guests at tables receive drinks "within two minutes of ordering," and that "all guests at the bar receive drinks within one minute of ordering."

"Service at the Café des Artistes is professional and complete, yet offered in a relaxed, caring, and friendly manner," the manual instructs. "It is important that you present a clean, caring, attractive, intelligent, and down-to-earth image of the restaurant at all times, and that you thoroughly inform yourself about our wine and food."

To further enhance their knowledge, employees serve each other between the lunch and dinner seatings. "Waiters become busboys, busboys become waiters," says Lang. "Waiters become managers and vice versa. Everybody gets to know everybody else's job. They get to sense it, feel it."

Customer comfort is at the core of the Lang manual, which warns that "anytime a guest needs to ask you for something, you've made a mistake. While this may seem strident in its philosophy, think of yourself as being the host of each table you serve. Your job is to help your guests relax and not need to ask for assistance. The only way to accomplish this is to figure out what they need, even before they know it themselves! This goes for bread and butter, water, more cocktails, club soda for spills, dessert menus, check presentation, etc. etc.!"

Lang says, "It is most important that customers be put at ease. It is a very strange phenomenon, but everyone, including those with a certain standing in society, feels a bit insecure when entering a restaurant. I want our staff to help eliminate that."

To that end, Lang sets the tone in a memorandum sent to the staff: "If there is a problem, we kiss every part of their body and go over half a dozen times to 'make nice,' etc. etc., instead of sending over a Great Dessert Plate without a word. This should be obvious!"

Lang isn't shy about the success of his service manual. "It teaches waitstaff how to fly," he says.

George Lang's welcoming presence (left) adds to the warmth of the Café experience.

are. I call the guys; they call me. I invite them to my home on their weekends off."

Although several of the Langs' younger managers, such as Henrick Parre and Ryan Buttner, have come to the Café from other restaurants or hotel schools, others, such as Susan Readwin, have graduated from the waitstaff. Most employees settle into the comfort of longevity at the Café, but a few do not. A prime example is the actor Brad Pitt, who put in some time as a waiter before going off to the movies.

"I began here in 1954, June 12," says Hiran Pagan. "I am a happy man. People ask for me. They request my tables. They show me their family pictures. I ask about their children. I served President Clinton when he came here. I asked him what he'd like to eat and he said, 'Whatever you eat.' "

Pagan, a bespectacled fellow with hair that seems a bit too red for his 63 years, adjusts the fruit and vegetable bowls on the baker's table display. "They call from Saudi Arabia. They call from London. They want Hiran when they come in. I have supported my wife and children and four grandchildren from here. A little while ago, I asked Mr. Lang when he was going to retire. He said, 'Never.' I told him, 'I'm with you, Mr. Lang.'"

Danny Kontotanasis has worked at the Café since 1972, and he knows precisely the size and number of Little Neck clams that Paul Newman will order when the actor is seated at one of his tables. He says he would not dream of waiting tables in any other restaurant. "I go to other places. I check details. We are much better than those other places," he says with pride. "All of us waiters, we are a group. We work together. We never have to look at each other. We just know how the other is going to act, and we know what Mr. Lang wants. You know, if he threw me out the

Most employees settle into life at the Café. An exception: The actor Brad Pitt, who put some time in as a waiter before going off to the movies.

front door, I would come in from the back. I will never leave."

Occasionally, waiters do leave in midstream. Such was the case when Abel Hamid Merchike, who was said to be happy in his work, became happier, even ecstatic. He won $1.6 million in the New York State Lottery and subsequently resigned, but not before working another six months at the Café.

How have the Langs kept their staff virtually intact over the years? Says George, "We give our people trust, we try to instill pride in what they do. You have to give them responsibility, courage, and confidence, and provide the foundation that will dictate how they will react under pressure, how they will improvise. You have to excite and stimulate them and give them a sense of high purpose. After all, a waiter, a person who serves, is in a noble profession."

This lofty doctrine of work is passed on to the Café des Artistes staff in meetings held between lunch and dinner, and in the Lang's server manual, which asks rhetorically, "What is great service?" then answers: "Simply put, great service is based on how well people feel they have been treated. Unlike great food, which you can see, smell, taste, and savor, great service is somewhat intangible. To us, great service is not about flamboyant tuxedos, table-side cooking, or lifting silver domes off hot food plates in unison. Rather, great service occurs when guests leave our restaurant convinced that someone risked going that extra step to make them happy. Great service happens when our guests are convinced in their hearts that we are on their side."

Which is how Vilmar Fagundes sees it. From a Portuguese family in Brazil, Fagundes, who prefers to be called "Mike," says that the message of care for customers is drummed into them by the Langs. "I learned a lot of things from Mr. Lang. I listen, and

Great service, right down to remembering drink preferences, turns customers into regulars at the Café.

"It is a very strange phenomenon, but everyone, including those with a certain standing in society, feels a bit insecure when entering a restaurant. I want our staff to help eliminate that." —*George Lang*

watch, and I decided that he was right." Fagundes was a waiter before Lang took over, and recalls that the previous owner, Charles Turner, "would close the Café on May thirty-first every year and not reopen until Labor Day." Turner, who was French, used the time to return to his native country.

"We're open all the time now, and I wouldn't change that," says Fagundes, adding his voice to the chorus of waitstaff who wouldn't consider leaving. "I don't think I would have met King Gustav of Sweden anywhere else, or Moshe Dayan. Not any-where else."

Jesus Robalino likes the thought that he came to work for the Café in 1975, "with Mr. Lang, actually two months after," and dis-covered the differences between working there and at his previ-ous job. "Mr. Lang wants us to be part of the restaurant, not just employees. We taste everything. I found I enjoyed myself. I still do. Different faces, different people, old customers, every day is exciting."

Robalino has enjoyed making sure that Shirley MacLaine gets the bottomless glass of water she wants with her meals, and serving John Travolta "right after he made *Saturday Night Fever*. He was more excited about being here than I was to serve him."

When the president of Ecuador, Rodrigo Boja, visited the restaurant, Robalino, who is from Ecuador, served the leader. "It was an honor," he says.

Ron Didner delights as well in the minutiae of his duties as general manager. "I have my grilled vegetables at 3:30 p.m. Then I check out the wine stock. The reservation book is done by 4:30. Then we have our staff meeting, where we go over table requests and our 'PX' list, which covers important regulars, spe-cial wines, specific food requests, and special cakes and desserts. We do our wine-tasting right after and begin seating by 5:30. We're full by six."

This restaurant that habitually turns visitors into regulars worked the same magic on an employee in one notable case.

A Different Kind of Spotlight

The allure of the Café is difficult to resist. Just ask waitress Lorraine Chevallier, who was a student at the Manhattan School of Music when she applied for a job at the Café in 1988. "I thought I'd be Beverly Sills," she recalls. " [But] it's so seductive

when you come in here. I've never left." Chevallier still sings—to her children. And her husband is a dramatic tenor, so her home is filled with music.

"I meet people here that I wouldn't ordinarily, who I sometimes recognize only when I get their credit card," Chevallier says. "Like Jonas Salk. What a nice man! And Edwin Newman. He came in and I asked him about his books. Next thing I knew, he brought them all in for me. Jules Pfieffer did a small line drawing for me one evening to say thank you. That's the kind of life I have here. I love it so much, I do double shifts."

Stellar service and an inviting atmosphere envelop guests at the Café.

While a waitress and bartender at the Café from 1953 to 1973, Clare Oesch saw to the perfection of martinis for the likes of Harry Reasoner and his successor as anchor for the *ABC Evening News,* Peter Jennings. Jennings has been quoted as saying that Oesch was "always an elegant presence at the bar."

Now in her eighties, Oesch is the Café's best customer. She has lived in an apartment in the Hotel des Artistes for more than 40 years, and every evening she comes downstairs to the restaurant, first for a cocktail at the end seat at the bar in the Christy Room, then for a walk around the restaurant to say hello to the scores of people who know her, and then for dinner. Like Hiran Pagan, this slim, white-haired woman, who has an apparently inexhaustible wardrobe of precisely cut colorful suits, regards the Café as "my life."

In her years at the restaurant, she served a broad swath of actors and politicians, musicians and brokers, dancers and athletes, including, she recalls well, Ava Gardner and John Glenn, "who treated me like a queen." She says with a smile that to this day, "a lot of my friends ask me to make reservations for them, and I do." When she dines, usually with a close friend, she has "a small piece of beef. I don't eat much. I come for the atmosphere."

One evening each January, the restaurant is closed, sold out to Clare's friends so they can give her a birthday party. "My apartment upstairs is where I sleep," she says. "the Café des Artistes is my home."

Café des Artistes

CHAPTER SEVEN

A Star-studded Cast Of Customers

On the evenings when they go to Lincoln Center for the ballet or the opera, Dr. Murray Budabin and his wife, Angelica, always eat early at the Café des Artistes. "Some nights we miss the first act, and you know, we don't care," Angelica confides. And why? "Because we like the Café so much," replies her husband.

Conversely, John William Gruber, who always eats alone at the bar in the Christy Room, will leave the opera early, well before the curtain calls, so he can be assured of his favorite seat.

Implicit is the feeling conveyed by the Budabins and Gruber that they enjoy not only the food at the Café, not only its familiarity and warmth, but its inherent theater.

Customers of the Café are an intensely loyal lot. Many have lunch or dinner among the murals four or five times a week. Others may just stop by for sweets and coffee after walks through Central Park. All seem to be creatures of happy habit who say they enjoy not only the restaurant's comforting food but its aura of romance.

It wasn't romance, however, that drew Toni Knox, then a resident of the Hotel des Artistes, to the Café one Thanksgiving in the late 1970s. Entertaining in her apartment, she suddenly realized that her big feast was on the verge of ruin because her gravy was a disaster. She grabbed a large pitcher and went downstairs, where it was obligingly filled with hot brown gravy. "My dinner was saved by the Café," says Knox. "I don't live over the restaurant anymore, but I still come here.

I have to. This is my home, this is my living room." And surely her auxiliary kitchen, she might add.

Over the years, of course, the Café has catered to thousands of famous diners. Rudolph Valentino had his regular table, as have later stars, such as Sidney Poitier, Glenn Close, Harrison Ford, Barbra Streisand, Robert DeNiro, and Jane Fonda. Jacqueline Kennedy Onassis always ordered a baked potato with caviar, and Danny DeVito likes the Café to make him ham-and-cheese sandwiches.

New York's mayors have always been regulars, from Jimmy Walker, a colorful fellow who was delighted when he was called a dandy, to the effusive Fiorello LaGuardia, to the staid John Lindsay. And from Ed Koch, who fancies himself a standup comedian, to Rudolph Giuliani, who does not. All have in common a high regard for the Café des Artistes.

Richard Burton and Peter O'Toole were regulars when performing on Broadway, and so today are Whoopi Goldberg, Sylvester Stallone, Meryl Streep, Michael Douglas, Michelle Pfieffer, Steven Spielberg, Ali McGraw, Richard Gere, Tom Hanks, and Nicole Kidman. Former New York Governor Hugh Carey, former Secretary of State Henry Kissinger, and former Senator Alphonse D'Amato come in often, just as they did while in office. So do Donald Trump and his ex-wife Ivana, both devoted customers before, during, and after their very public marriage. Al Pacino, a man of simple wants, loves the Café's vanilla ice cream. Lauren Bacall more often than not has a Caesar salad with fresh romaine, and Hume Cronyn is a longtime fan of the calf's liver with bacon and onions.

Janos Siess, in his years as waiter and manager, served a virtual who's who of entertainers, artists, athletes, politicians, and others with familiar names or faces. He will, at

Chef Thomas Ferlesch unwinds in the Parlor with artist LeRoy Nieman.

At a special dessert-themed marriage proposal, a woman was presented with a dessert menu that read, "Pecan Pie, Crème Brulée, Michele Will You Marry Me? Charlie."

Romantic Proposals

*L*ike many regulars, there is one couple who have a special reason for being loyal to the Café des Artistes. According to Janos Siess, a retired manager at the Café, it all started when the man phoned for a dinner reservation, confiding that he intended to propose to his date that evening over dessert.

"We have lots of proposals, anniversaries, engagements, and birthdays, all kinds of celebrations," Siess says, "but this man wanted a special cake. They were at a back table, and when it came time for dessert, he said to the woman, 'Let's have a great dessert.' She said 'No,' because she seemed satisfied with her dinner. He said, 'Let's.' She demurred again but finally agreed. Our waiter ran to the bar and brought back a lovely little cake with icing that said, 'Will you marry me?'

"When she said yes, I brought out another cake I had made, with icing reading, "Thank you, darling. I love you.' That was for him. He was as surprised as she was."

At another special dessert-themed proposal, a woman was presented with a dessert menu that read, "Pecan Pie, Crème Brûlée with Caramel Sauce, Michele Will You Marry Me? Charlie, Vienna Fudge Torte, Pear Cranberry Tart." A grin crosses Siess's face as he asks, "Can you guess which dessert she picked?"

Another suitor chose to top off the meal in a different way. "The gentleman proposed," Siess says, "and when the lady accepted, we took them to the front of the restaurant so she could look out at the convertible Alfa Romeo he had bought her as an engagement present. They drove away with a complimentary bottle of Dom Perignon."

James Earl Jones, Peter Falk, and Larry King share a liking for the Cafe's pot-au-feu.

the drop of a reservation slip, recite a litany of them and their special wants. "Madonna likes that back table behind the bar, so she can be very private. She likes our fruit plate and endive, *loves* endive. Paul Newman? He likes that seat at the end of the banquette in the front dining room, right under the *Spring* mural."

Siess says that newsman Peter Jennings would often come in after evening broadcasts and sit at the bar playing dollar poker. "Howard Cosell came in a lot, sometimes with Muhammad Ali, and they were never pretentious, always gentlemen. You can say that about Mick Jagger, too, a quiet man who usually ordered our black bean soup and salmon Benedict at brunch."

It is possible for those well known to be unassuming at the Café. Lang delights in one exceptional tale of non-recognition. "Just after we opened in 1975, a dignified gentleman in black tie called me over to his table and complimented me on the resurrection of the Café. Then he added, 'Just one thing, Mr. Lang. How can you allow people to come in so terribly dressed as the ones at that table in the corner?' He was pointing toward the round table directly next to the entrance and, true enough, there was a party of eight where the men especially looked rather casual, in open-neck shirts and unpressed slacks. Not able to resist a perfect squelch, I said to this gentlemanly gentleman, 'Sir, I shall go over and tell Sir Laurence Olivier to dress more properly next time.'"

Celebrities often have their favorite dishes, and those for whom the Café is an outpost of comfort and familiarity are sure to find them there. James Earl Jones, Peter Falk, and Larry King dote on the pot-au-feu, and perhaps the only thing that Sean Connery might have in common with New York's Governor George Pataki is a love for the Café's osso buco. Maya Angelou, Placido Domingo, Morgan Freeman, and Liam Neeson come in for the rack of lamb, and Demi Moore favors egg-white omelettes.

Celebrities or no, the Café has come to be a place for special occasions, birthdays, the completion of a Woody Allen movie, anniversaries, Tony Award celebrations, and engagements.

■

For special occasions, ornate menus are prepared, like the one at right for a benefit dinner.

Café des Artistes

A Gastronomic Divertimento
for the
American Austrian Benefit
with the Vienna Philharmonic

Menu

Foie Gras with its Cracklings & Port Wine Aspic
served on toasted Brioche

♪ ♪ ♪

accompanied by Gundel'own
Tokaji "Harslevelü"-1993

♪ ♪ ♪

Chef Thomas Ferlesch presents

Beef-Goulash with Nockerl
and home-style Essig-Gurken

Egri Cabernet 1993
from the Lauder / Lany Vineyards

Traditional Viennese Milchrahmstrudel

Schlumberger Vienna Brut Champagne

Sunday, March 9, 1997.   New York City

Occasionally, the Langs prepare special menus, usually for longtime customers and friends. The menu on the evening of August 14, 1987, was indeed special, a printed birth announcement for the Langs' son, Simon.

The warmth of the Café is such that patrons sometimes treat each other like family. Lang tells of coming into the Café one evening to begin his rounds of the tables, when he overheard a couple thanking frequent customer Donald Hillman for the use of a jacket.

"Later, I asked Donald what the story was," Lang recalls. "He said he'd overheard this gentleman, Frederic Schwartz, speaking with our manager, who was regretfully explaining that jackets were required after 5 p.m. While the Café does have a number of them available, that night all were in use. So Hillman, a resident of the Hotel des Artistes, offered the gentleman one of his jackets, if the couple would wait while he went up to his apartment to get one." Schwartz wore the jacket, the couple enjoyed their dinner, and the jacket was being returned when Lang happened by.

Schwartz subsequently wrote a letter of gratitude to Hillman, who passed it along to Lang. "Thank you for the use of your coat," it began. "I first met the woman I was taking out 25 years ago. We recently re-met. After a few dates over a couple of months, I decided that the Café des Artistes would be the place to make my big move. So I really do appreciate the use of your coat and the generosity of your spirit. She liked the coat and so did I. It worked, and we went to work very late today, together at last."

Another evening, Lang recalls, he was greeting regular guests when "a man excitedly asked me if I would sit down so he could tell me a story. I never sit with guests, but I stood by him as he told me a story that began 21 years ago, when he was having dinner with his wife at the Café. He said, "She told me we were going to have a baby. This is her.' The gentleman gestured toward the young woman across from him, seated next to his wife. 'Tonight, our daughter can enjoy

■

Celebrities or no, regular customers often come in for special dishes prepared as only the Café can.

Jacqueline Kennedy Onassis always ordered a baked potato with caviar, and Danny DeVito likes the Café for ham and cheese sandwiches.

THE PRESIDENT CALLS

*I*n the case of some very special guests, the Café is forced to adapt quickly, which is not easily done in a restaurant that usually plays to full houses and is booked weeks in advance. But this call came from the White House. President Clinton was to be in town the evening of October 23, 1995, and would dearly love to dine at the Café des Artistes—with nine friends.

Says Lang, "The secret of success is to accept the impossible, do without the indispensable, and bear the intolerable." First, he had to accept the impossibility of providing three tables at 9 p.m., because the restaurant was already fully booked. He phoned old customers who had reservations, asked them to come earlier or later, and added several smaller tables to the dining room.

But where to put the president? "None of those making the arrangements could decide which was the best table," says Lang, "so we seated him in the main dining room on the banquette, and the Secret Service blocked off the windows to the street."

The menu consisted of house specialties, offered family style so the president and his guests could serve themselves. Hiran Pagan, who has a thick scrapbook of photos showing him with the rich and famous, was assigned to the table to start the party off with platters of charcuterie, fresh asparagus, and salmon. Later came the swordfish paillard, long-bone veal chops, grilled quail, and one of the Langs' festive dishes from the Austro-Hungarian empire, venison *pörkölt* with spätzle and a cucumber salad.

The meal was a success, Lang reports, adding that at one point during the feast the president drew him aside and said, " 'George, the standard line about New York is that the only thing permanent is change, but I guess the people who keep saying that have not been to the Café des Artistes.' He also told me that he loved our macadamia nut torte."

Recalling that evening, Lang interjects his personal definition of a great restaurant experience: "You've succeeded when a warm glow radiates from the faces of your guests." He says that "when the president and his guests left the Café des Artistes, I knew we had succeeded."

the same escargots that we had that night, at the same table,' he said. I neglected to ask him what he'd paid in 1978, but I felt that a bottle of champagne was definitely in order."

The loyalty of the customers and the staff was put to the test just two days before Christmas in 1997, when a short in a power panel caused a fire in the Café's kitchen. Flames and smoke spread through ducts up one floor but were contained by the quick response of truckfuls of city firemen. Although the dining area was undamaged, the restaurant was forced to close for more than four months. The staff spent virtually all of their time canceling reservations,

It was a great day for the Langs and their son, Simon, when President Bill Clinton came to dine.

particularly from people for whom a meal at the Café des Artistes had become a Christmas tradition.

Lang announced to the staff that all employees would be kept on full salary until the reopening. "I told them they are family," Lang says. "I said this has nothing to do with unions, we were just going to do it." He says that after making this announcement to the assembled staff, "some cheered, some cried. Everyone came over and kissed me. It was incredible."

After the kitchen was restored, the Langs set about restoring residual damage to the Café's social and culinary fabric. Tastings went on. New menus were devised. Personal notes were sent to every tenant of the Hotel des Artistes, inviting them to an afternoon party and mentioning that the cooperative owners would be given preference, and complimentary champagne, should they desire to reserve tables for reopening day, May 1, 1998. All the restaurant's steady customers were advised of the date. The Langs suggested that managers buy a bottle of wine for good customers on what was to be called First Guests Night.

The reopening was festive indeed, for those who reserved and for eight special guests who needed no reservations: The first four of the 121 firemen who had come running into the Café on the afternoon of the fire were invited, along with their wives. Seated in the Christy Room, they ate and drank as guests of the Café and were toasted by the other diners.

It was more than simply a gesture, says Lang. Rather, "It was our Café family's way, mine and Jenifer's, that of our dining room staff, and our chef and his cooks, of saying thank you, symbolically, to our city's Fire Department."

Customers of the Café are intensely loyal—some dine among the murals four or five times a week.

Café des Artistes

CHAPTER EIGHT

THE CAFÉ, VIEWS AND REVIEWS

*I*t will cause no eyebrow to raise to note that the Café des Artistes has long been praised by restaurant critics and their fellow food reviewers and essayists. Critics for newspapers, because of the immediacy of their medium, are surely the most influential of judges, and quite often their opinions can ensure a restaurant's success or presage that it will flounder. Somewhat less impactful are critics for magazines, who must come out with weekly, monthly, or quarterly assessments.

It is fair to say that gastronomic critics from newspapers and magazines the world over have looked favorably upon the Café over the quarter of a century since its rejuvenation. And they have been joined by the publishers of guidebooks, by those who collate reviews into restaurant guides, and by magazines that list current and recurring readers' favorites. Parts of motion pictures have been filmed in the Café, and it has been embraced lovingly by TV and radio. Its murals and its tables have even provided occasional settings for novels and nonfiction writings.

The early tone was set by *The New York Times* when John Canaday, the *Times* art critic turned restaurant reviewer, wrote that the restaurant's interior was "not like any other in New York and one of the most attractive in the city." Writing in 1975, little more than a month after the Café's reopening, he suggested that its refurbishment was "a strong argument for having your face lifted if you had a good one to begin with." The nude murals, Canaday wrote with feeling, were "very pink within their very green copses, like peppermint mousse on beds of spinach." As for the food, Canaday raved about the "strength of the excellent dishes we had à la carte," noting also that "service is excellent and there is a generally happy air about the place." He awarded it three out of a possible four stars and suggested, "If the Café des Artistes can keep up its present standard of high performance, it should really be four."

The New York Times rave was followed quickly by that of Eugenia Sheppard in *The New York Post.* Sheppard, often credited with being the first of the true food critics while at *The New York Herald Tribune*, wrote, "The sleeper among New York restaurants is the recently reborn Café des Artistes." *The Village Voice* noted, "If you feel New York is slipping, the present renaissance of Café des Artistes may single-handedly revive your spirit."

Hosannas were sung in the influential *Gourmet* magazine as well, by Jay Jacobs, perhaps the most erudite, thorough, and knowledgeable of New

John Canaday of **The New York Times** *raved about the Café's cuisine, while* **The New Yorker** *(right) took a different tack.*

York's gastronomic critics. He called the Café "a born again phenomenon" with a menu comprising "the most innovative food in the city." He went on at length about the authenticity of the Café's *bourride* as well as its other dishes rooted in the French countryside, and concluded, "In a few short months, the Café des Artistes has outstripped Lang's original concept of its function. The restaurant was far too good to remain a mere neighborhood haunt, and it now attracts a goodly share of celebrated personages from all walks of life and all parts of the nation. It's a happy, exciting, beautiful place, and I can't imagine how any of us—Howard Chandler Christy's marcelled *filles du bois* included—could possibly get along without it."

Over the years *New York* magazine, with Gael Greene leading the parade, has weighed in with hoorahs of pleasure over the Café's food and look. "The Café is a joy," Greene wrote. "George has accomplished a subtle miracle. Some of the nudes are gone, passageways have been banished, windows thrown open to the street...a major overhaul, yet all patina is skillfully restored. Enter and retreat into a gentler era, a Viennese operetta." Later, the magazine, in a "Tops in Town" recommendation, lauded a special dessert when it was placed on the menu. "One of the most attractive desserts around is Mr. Christy's Ice Cream Palette.... The plate is shaped like an artist's palette, decorated with ice creams and sorbet, chocolate mousse, whipped cream, berries, walnuts, and hot fudge."

The Telegraph of London has praised the Café, as did that ubiquitous columnist, the late Herb Caen, who wrote in *The San Francisco Chronicle*, "Best show in town: brunch at Café des Artistes followed by Central Park on the first fine Sunday in May."

Over the years, the New York *Daily News* has continually recommended the Café. Its critic, Daniel Young, suggested that it would be "where Fred Astaire and Ginger Rogers would go on Valentine's Day."

Daniel Young, restaurant critic for the *Daily News*, has suggested that the Café is "where Fred Astaire and Ginger Rogers would go on Valentine's Day."

Tops, Time and Again

Many publications have afforded the Café des Artistes a seemingly permanent spot on their most favored restaurant lists. The *Zagat Survey* annually lists the Café on its roster of most visited New York eateries. Similarly, *Fine Dining* magazine placed the Café in its Hall of Fame, and *Food & Wine* has set it into a

diadem as one of the jewels of romantic restaurants around the United States. *Condé Nast Traveler*, annually, it seems, places the Café on its list of distinguished American restaurants.

Which guidebook has not recommended the Café des Artistes? Quite probably not a single one. The *Mobil Travel Guide, New York Access, Fodor's, Frommer's, The Berlitz Travelers Guide*, New York restaurant guides from Mimi Sheraton and Bryan Miller, *Passport Guides*, and the *Bantam Travel Guides* have all urged visitors and natives alike to go to this romantic little restaurant.

Asparagus is a perennial Café favorite.

An Asparagus
Menu
For Friends

Asparagus Crisped in Beer Batter
with a Springtime Crème Fraiche Dip

Chef John's Spicy Seafood
and Asparagus Risotto

Green Asparagus from Salinas
Family Style

Mr. Christy's Ice Cream Palette
(Tony.) — one Asparagus

"The Café is a joy... Enter and retreat into a gentler era, a Viennese operetta." —*Gael Greene,* New York *magazine*

Newsday called it a "grand café," where "nymphs smile agelessly behind the tables of New Yorkers from all walks of life who treat this restaurant as a home away from home." The Café has also been written about in *Architectural Digest, Travel & Leisure, Bon Appétit, The Hollywood Reporter,* and *Quest.*

Its location, its felicitous look, and its romantic aura have all made the Café a sought-after setting for motion pictures, as well. Scenes from Woody Allen's *Manhattan Murder Mystery* were filmed there, as were parts of *The Fan,* starring Lauren Bacall. The film *9 1/2 Weeks,* starring Mickey Rourke and Kim Basinger, a regular customer along with her husband, Alec Baldwin, features the Café. Bette Midler, Goldie Hawn, and Diane Keaton filmed scenes for their *First Wives Club* there.

Nor has the Café been neglected by the financial community. *Forbes* suggests that its murals alone are worth a trip, and *Crain's New York Business* opined, "If there is a more welcoming setting with a more appealing menu than Café des Artistes, I have not found it." *The Wall Street Journal* quotes the *Zagat Survey* , which describes the restaurant as a rendezvous where "you could fall in love with your IRS agent during an audit."

The Café makes a cameo appearance in James B. Stewart's book *Den of Thieves,* which traces the machinations of some of the more suspect stock traders of the 1970s. Stewart places two of his subjects, the slick Ivan Boesky and John Mulheren, a young but exceedingly clever trader of stock options, at the "home to one of the city's venerable eateries, the Café des Artistes," where they discuss the stock market's coming takeover boom. When the waiter comes to take their orders, Boesky says, "I'll have every entrée."

As the book reports, "When the food arrived, the waiter wheeled a table next to them. On it were eight featured dishes of the day. Boesky looked them over carefully, circled the table, took one bite of each. He selected one, and sent the rest back."

Says George Lang, "It happened just as it was written." And though Ivan Boesky was later to go to prison for his financial misdeeds, Lang never insisted that the man's prison sentence be lengthened on charges of lack of respect for food.

Many neighbors use the parlor as an extension of their living rooms.

A Novelist's Dream Come True

The Café's long history and landmark-like status make it a splendid setting for romance and intrigue in novel form. Katherine Neville, for example, in her suspense novel *A Calculated Risk*, has her hero settle into his Manhattan hotel room and read a message given to him by the desk clerk. It says, "Your favorite restaurant. Noon." Which is? The Café des Artistes, naturally. Neville's hero describes the Café as resembling "something from Paris during the expatriation of the literati...nude coquettes with golden limbs, unexpectedly peeping from the dense foliage—all done in a mish-mash style combining Watteau, Gibson Girl, and Douanier Rousseau—real Big Apple kitsch."

In the murder mystery *Blood on the Street*, Annette Meyers's investigative heroine, Wetzon, arrives for dinner at the Café des Artistes and finds herself among "types that might have stepped out of an F. Scott Fitzgerald novel" as she makes her way to her date, one Alton Pinkus, who is "sitting in a booth just past the bar talking to a distinguished, balding man, compact in a good tweed sports jacket. They both rose to greet her, and Alton introduced her to George Lang, the owner of Café des Artistes."

From the bar they are taken to their table at the banquette against the front windows, and Wetzon orders the salmon four ways as an appetizer, then grilled swordfish with a tomato olive coulis and a 1963 Montrachet. She finds "the food, the wine, the romance of the restaurant bewitching," and as they ate, "they were interrupted three more times by people she didn't know, once by the director of the Metropolitan, whose name she recognized, and finally by Ed Koch, an ex-mayor of the city, who heartily recommended The Great Bonaparte for dessert."

In *Someone Is Killing the Great Chefs of America*, Nan and Ivan Lyons place their protagonists, Natasha and Alec, in the Café because it "was the perfect place in which to fall in love. Alec allowed himself to be carried away, as did everyone, by the Howard Chandler Christy murals of cavorting buxom beauties, the sparkle of crystal and silver, the patina of old wood, and the gentle purr of a sophisticated clientele." For her part, Natasha is greeted with open arms by "George Lang, the Mozart of the restaurant business."

The Café has been the setting for numerous intrigues in both motion pictures and novels.

Fresh fruit is an important part of the menu at the Café.

Café des Artistes

CHAPTER NINE

TASTINGS AND TASTES

It was time for one of the tastings that play a critical role in creating the cuisine of the Café des Artistes. Chef Thomas Ferlesch had devised seven new dishes that he wanted considered for the Café's menu. In attendance were George and Jenifer Lang, along with the restaurant's general manager, Ron Didner, three of his assistant managers, and several members of the waitstaff.

"The ideas for the dishes come from all of us," Jenifer says, "and Thomas executes them for what I call our parliamentary tastings. Everybody is invited to taste and to comment."

The tastings, which take place every three weeks or so, are held in the restaurant's main front dining room, after the luncheon service but well before the beginning of dinner. On this occasion, several tables had been freshened with linen. Napkins were layered in piles, dishes were stacked, silverware was laid out, and at precisely 3:30, the Langs called for the dishes to be brought out, one at a time.

Ferlesch appeared with two plates holding thick slices of *tête de veau* dressed with a basil vinaigrette. It was not very different from a dish already on the menu, usually served with an onion relish or breaded and sautéed. Ferlesch liked this new version for its somewhat chewy tex-

"The ideas come from all of us. Everybody is invited to taste and to comment." —*Jenifer Lang*

ture and suggested that it was more like a terrine. The consensus was that it was sufficiently different to try, but the vinaigrette might benefit from the punch of a bit more vinegar. The tables were cleared by the waiters, who were also tasting.

Next were soft crepes, looking like a cross between beggars' purses and Chinese soup dumplings, filled with minced chanterelle mushrooms and served with a sauce redolent of paprika and sour cream. These received immediate, unanimous approval, with Jenifer Lang smiling between mouthfuls and saying, "Put them on the menu tomorrow." The crepes were followed by an unusual Ferlesch contrivance: sliced beef cheeks with thin green beans, the *haricots verts* of the French kitchen, topped with a sauce of shallots and dill. This too was deemed excellent, with the cheeks a nice chew and the dressing bringing raves from everyone.

Judgments varied on the next preparation, a napoleon of sliced fresh and smoked buffalo mozzarella, layered with slices of roasted peppers and beefsteak tomatoes, accompanied by thin, crisply fried pieces of phyllo as a crackerlike garnish. Some samplers found the fresh mozzarella tasteless but liked the smoked; others thought all of the layers should be sliced more thinly. A vote was taken, and George announced the

Thanks to periodic tastings, the Café serves an incredible variety of new dishes.

results. "More like it than not. I think a modified version will go onto the menu soon." As it turned out, the dish was in place within two days.

Perhaps Ferlesch's most ambitious preparation was a classic sauerbraten made from braised shoulder of beef, its sauce perfectly tart. He set it out with slices of white dumplings ("like my mother made in Vienna") that were dressed with a fine, grainy paste composed of fried bread crumbs and butter. It was in the style of Bohemia, Ferlesch said, and it brought forth another unanimous burst of enthusiasm. A marvelous dish from any standpoint, it was agreed. "A plus," said Jenifer. "We'll work on the menu wording and get it to you by tomorrow."

Two desserts followed. In the first, an apple strudel Viennese style, the cooked apples were encased in a thin crust quite unlike the thicker one usually associated with this classic. Again, there was a unanimous verdict that it belonged on the menu, somewhere between the toasted orange savarin and the Linzer torte. The verdict was the same for the second dessert, Ferlesch's version of a typical American shortcake recipe: basically shortbread scones smothered with a blueberry compote and topped with a scoop of blueberry sorbet. Perfect, with one minor cavil. "It's too big; it looks like a steakhouse dessert," George said. Ferlesch agreed that it should be done on a smaller scale.

It is from such tastings that the Café's menu continues to evolve. There are, to be sure, the restaurant's classics, familiar dishes that its customers demand, but change comes with each printing of the day's menu. This practice is tangible evidence of the Langs' philosophy of maintaining "subtle continuity" at the Café des Artistes.

Who could resist a dessert like peanut butter pie (left)?

RECIPES

Seafood Gazpacho, 67th Street Style

This "drinkable food," as the ancient Greeks called gazpacho, has many variations, some with almonds, some mixed with mayonnaise, and some, as in the Café's version, flavored with seafood.

Serves 8 to 10

2 1/2 pounds ripe red tomatoes, peeled, seeded, and chopped

1 cup coarsely chopped Bermuda onion

1/2 cup chopped green pepper

1/2 cup chopped carrot

1 clove garlic, peeled

5 cups tomato juice

1/3 cup red wine vinegar

Salt and freshly ground black pepper to taste

2 tablespoons olive oil

8 ounces tiny shrimp, peeled, deveined, and lightly cooked

Dash of Louisiana-type hot sauce

1/4 cup chopped fresh dill

6 medium scallions, white part only, washed and cut into 1/4-inch dice

1 large cucumber, peeled, seeded, and cut into 1/4-inch dice

1 cup freshly toasted croutons

Garnish

1. Chop tomatoes, onion, green pepper, carrots, and garlic in a food processor until the mixture takes on a rough texture.

2. Stir in tomato juice and vinegar, and season with salt and pepper. Whisk in olive oil. Chill for at least 3 hours.

3. Add shrimp. Adjust seasoning with hot sauce, and serve sprinkled with dill in chilled bowls, with crocks of scallion, cucumber, and croutons on the side.

Pear Champagne

Lucius Beebe, the late, great journalist, reported the gustatory and social glamour of champagne concoctions in the 1920s, when the smart set first discovered them. The following champagne cocktail made its debut at the Café in 1977, when it was served to a pear-loving friend.

Serves 4

1/4 cup sugar

1/4-inch-thick slice fresh ginger, the
    diameter of a quarter

1 fresh Bartlett, anjou, or Comice pear,
    peeled and cored

2 tablespoons Williams pear brandy

Dry champagne

1. In a saucepan, combine sugar, 1/2 cup water, and ginger. Bring to a boil. Stand the pear upright in the liquid. Cover and simmer until almost cooked. The fruit should remain slightly crunchy.
2. Quarter the pear and place each quarter in a champagne glass. Divide the pear brandy among the glasses and fill with champagne. Serve immediately.

Lima Bean and Zucchini Potage with Parsley Pesto

George and Jenifer Lang wholeheartedly agree with Voltaire, who said that the best-written book is a recipe for soup.

Serves 8

1/4 cup olive oil

1/2 cup chopped onion

1/2 cup diced carrot

1/2 cup diced celery

1 cup diced zucchini

1 cup tomato concassé (peeled, seeded, and chopped)

1 cup lima beans (fresh or frozen)

10 cups chicken stock

1 tablespoon minced fresh basil

1 teaspoon fresh thyme

1 bay leaf

1/2 cup potatoes, peeled and diced

Salt to taste

1. Heat olive oil in a large casserole. Add onions, carrots, and celery. Cover, and sweat vegetables over low heat for 10 minutes.
2. Add zucchini, lima beans, tomato concassé, chicken stock, basil, thyme, and bay leaf. Bring to a boil, then add potatoes. Lower heat and simmer 20 minutes. Add salt to taste. Remove bay leaf before serving.
3. To serve: Put a spoonful of Parsley Pesto (*see* recipe page 137) in each soup plate, then ladle the hot soup over it. Serve remaining Parsley Pesto at the table. This meal is delicious with garlic bread.

Parsley Pesto

2 bunches Italian parsley, stems removed

1/2 cup blanched and chopped
  fresh spinach

4-6 cloves garlic

1/4 cup grated Parmigiano-Reggiano
  cheese

1/2 cup French or Italian extra-virgin olive oil

Salt and freshly ground pepper to taste

Mix all ingredients in a food processor.

Moules Honfleur

Cleaning the mussels thoroughly is essential for any recipe, unless you like sand in your seafood. Honfleur is a quaint little port in Normandy, and mussels are served in this manner in several of its restaurants.

Serves 4 as a main course

56 large mussels, scrubbed well, and with
  beards removed

1 1/2 cups dry white wine

1 cup heavy cream

4 tablespoons unsalted butter, cut into pieces

1 tablespoon plus 1 teaspoon chopped shallots

1 tablespoon plus 1 teaspoon chopped
  fresh parsley

2 teaspoons freshly ground white pepper

1. Combine all ingredients in a large saucepan. Cook covered, over medium high heat, stirring once or twice, until mussels just begin to open (about 3 to 5 minutes). With a slotted spoon, remove mussels to a large bowl; cover and keep warm.

2. Cook mussel liquid over high heat for 10 minutes. Divide mussels and liquid among four heated shallow soup plates and serve.

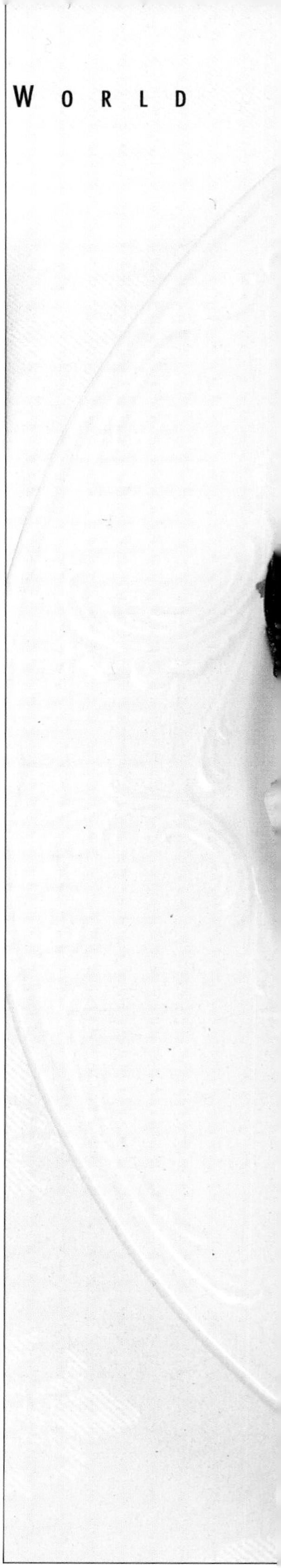

Crispy Soft-Shell Crabs with Ginger, Scallion, and Cilantro

Soft-shell crabs should be purchased the day you plan to serve them.

Serves 4

8 soft-shell crabs

1 lemon, halved

Salt to taste

3 eggs, beaten

1 1/2 cups flour

1 1/2 cups Japanese
  bread crumbs

Vegetable oil for sautéeing

1 1/2 cups sliced scallions
  (slice the green part thicker,
  the white part thinner)

3/4 cup cilantro leaves

1/4 cup julienne of fresh ginger

Sliced jalapeño pepper to taste

1/4 cup soy sauce

3 tablespoons sesame oil

1 tablespoon honey

1. Season soft-shell crabs with lemon juice and salt.

2. Dust each crab in flour, dip in beaten egg, then coat with Japanese bread crumbs.

3. Pan fry crabs on both sides until crispy and golden brown. Keep warm while preparing the sauce.

4. In another large sauté pan, heat 2 tablespoons vegetable oil and sauté scallion, cilantro, ginger, and jalapeño over high heat for a minute or two. Pour the soy sauce, sesame oil, and honey into the sauté pan, stir, and cook for 20 more seconds. Spoon sauce over soft-shell crabs. Serve immediately.

Smoked Salmon Benedict, Café des Artistes

Lemmuel Benedict, a Wall Street stockbroker, used to order toast, a few slices of crisp bacon, two poached eggs, and a gooseneck of hollandaise sauce at the Waldorf Astoria's Men's Bar. Chef Oscar Tschirky of the Waldorf eventually exchanged the toast for English muffin and the bacon for ham, then added truffle slices and a few drops of *glace de viande,* a concentrated meat extract. The Café, in turn, made changes to accommodate smoked salmon–loving eggs Benedict addicts.

Serves 4

8 eggs

4 English muffins, split

16 thin slices smoked salmon
   (approximately 1/2 pound)

Fresh watercress or other green herb for garnish

Béarnaise Sauce (*see* recipe below)

1. Fill a medium-size saucepan with water, approximately 5 inches deep, and add the juice of 1 lemon (this will help the eggs coagulate). Heat to simmering.

2. One at a time, break the eggs into the water, trying to keep them as separate as possible. Poach for 3 minutes.

3. While the eggs are poaching, toast English muffins under a preheated broiler. Put two slices of smoked salmon on each toasted muffin half.

4. Using a slotted spoon, remove the eggs as soon as they are firm. Drain well and place one on top of each muffin half on warm serving plates, allowing two per portion.

5. Coat each egg with Béarnaise Sauce, garnish with watercress or other green herb sprig, and serve at once.

Béarnaise Sauce

2 tablespoons chopped fresh tarragon leaves

3 tablespoons tarragon vinegar (white wine
   vinegar may be substituted)

2 tablespoons finely chopped shallots

1 teaspoon freshly ground black pepper

1 1/3 cups dry white wine

6 egg yolks

2 cups unsalted butter, diced and at
   room temperature

Salt and cayenne pepper to taste

Juice of 1 lemon plus more fresh lemon juice
   to taste

1. Combine tarragon, vinegar, shallots, pepper, and wine in a large saucepan. Bring to a boil over medium-high heat and reduce to 1/4 cup of liquid. Remove from heat and let cool.

2. To complete the sauce, combine egg yolks with 2 tablespoons water in the top of a double

boiler and whisk until lemony in color. Continue whisking over simmering water until the mixture is light and fluffy. Add pieces of butter, one at a time, whisking until completely incorporated. Strain through a fine sieve into a small bowl. Season with salt, cayenne pepper, and lemon juice to taste. Whisk in cooled tarragon reduction. Keep warm.

Tartar Steak

You can invent relishes and garnishes for this dish. The Café uses a tablespoon each of diced tomatoes, minced onion, and capers, served in little cups made of onion lavers. You can also serve garnishes in hollowed-out lemon halves.

Serves 4

3 egg yolks, lightly beaten

1 1/2 teaspoons high-quality curry powder

1/4 cup Dijon mustard

2 ounces anchovy fillets, drained and coarsely chopped

1/4 cup capers (small size), rinsed and drained

1/4 cup finely chopped Bermuda onion

1/2 cup toasted pine nuts

1/4 teaspoon freshly ground black pepper

24 ounces freshly ground lean sirloin steak

2 tablespoons vegetable oil

1. Combine eggs yolks, curry powder, and mustard in a large mixing bowl and blend well. Add anchovies, capers, onions, pine nuts, and pepper, and mix together.

2. Add ground sirloin and thoroughly combine all ingredients. Do not overmix. Adjust seasoning to taste, using more curry powder or pepper. Divide mixture into four portions, and form each into an oval patty.

3. Optional: To lightly toast the steaks, heat oil in a large frying pan until it is very hot and begins to swirl in the pan. Carefully place each patty in the hot oil. Quickly sear patties over high heat, just long enough to brown—no more than 1 minute on each side. Remove patties from pan, and drain on paper towels to absorb excess fat. Serve at once.

Bourride with Aïoli

A fish casserole, Provencal-style

Bourride is a second cousin to bouillabaisse, a soup-stew enriched by two important staples of Provence: very fresh garlic and local olive oil. Chef Thomas Ferlesch's version is based on *bourrides* he has tasted at homes and restaurants in and around Marseilles.

Serves 4

1 cup extra-virgin olive oil (French,
  if possible)

1/2 cup diced onion

1/2 cup julienne of leek (white part only)

1/2 cup diced fennel

1/2 cup diced celery

1/2 cup diced carrot

3 cloves garlic

2 cups white wine

1 cup diced tomato

Splash of Pernod

1 teaspoon saffron threads

Bouquet garni of bay leaves, fresh thyme,
  and Italian parsley wrapped in cheese cloth

2 quarts fish stock (preferably made from
  bones or head of halibut, grouper, snapper,
  or a combination of all)

Kosher salt to taste

Freshly ground black pepper to taste

2 pounds boneless fish fillet and shellfish
  (*see* note)

Zest of one orange

Note: Types of seafood that can be used for preparation (choose at least three): halibut, eel, monkfish, grouper, cod, snapper, shrimp, scallops, mussels, and clams.

1. Put 1/2 cup of the olive oil into a deep heavy casserole over medium heat. Sauté onions, leeks, fennel, celery, carrots, and garlic for approximately 10 minutes, stirring. Vegetables must not change color.

2. Add white wine, tomatoes, Pernod, saffron, and bouquet garni, and cook for another 10 minutes.

3. Add fish stock and bring to a boil. Let cook approximately 15 minutes, until vegetables are soft.

4. Remove bouquet garni and put liquid in blender. Blend until smooth, then add remaining olive oil. Salt and pepper to taste.

5. Bring liquid to a boil. Add orange zest. Add fish and simmer until fish is cooked (approximately 5 minutes).

6. Remove cooked fish from liquid and place in serving dish; keep warm. Put fish broth into a bowl and whisk in 1/2 cup aïoli (*see* recipe page 145) until smooth and creamy. Pour sauce over fish. Reheat if necessary, but do not bring to a boil. Serve with remaining aïoli on the side.

Saffron Aïoli

2 cups cold mayonnaise (preferably
   homemade)

1 garlic clove, finely minced

1/2 lemon, seeds removed

Kosher salt to taste

Freshly ground black pepper to taste

Cayenne pepper to taste

2 pinches saffron threads

1. Combine the mayonnaise and garlic. Squeeze the lemon over the mixture, stir, and add salt and cayenne to taste.

2. In a small saucepan, simmer the saffron and 1/4 cup water until reduced to 1 teaspoon of liquid. Whisk into the saffron essence. Chill.

Cod and Crabmeat Cakes

Serves 6

1 pound jumbo lump crabmeat

2 pounds baked cod fillet

1 1/2 cups diced sweet peppers:
   a mixture of yellow, green, and red

1 bunch minced scallions, white part only

Juice of 3 limes

3/4 cup mayonnaise

3/4 cup Dijon mustard

2 eggs, beaten

Salt and pepper to taste

1 cup Japanese bread crumbs

Vegetable oil for sautéeing

1. Using your fingers, gently combine cooled off codfish and crabmeat. Add peppers, scallions, salt, pepper, and lime juice. Mix well.

2. Add mayonnaise, mustard, and eggs. Mix well. Add enough of the bread crumbs to bind mixture. Let stand for 1 hour.

3. Form mixture into cakes; coat each one on both sides with bread crumbs. Sauté in hot oil until brown and crisp. Serve with salsa or guacamole.

Sturgeon Milanese Style

Who knows why sturgeon is served almost exclusively smoked when, cooked fresh, the texture and pale white color of this fish recall a cutlet of especially young veal.

Serves 4

8 thin slices of lake sturgeon (about
   3 ounces each)

Salt and freshly ground black pepper

All-purpose flour for dredging

3 eggs, lightly beaten

1 1/2 cups freshly made bread crumbs

1/2 cup olive oil or clarified butter

4 tablespoons unsalted butter

2 lemons, halved

1. Season sturgeon slices on both sides with salt and pepper. Dust slices in flour, shaking off excess. Dip in egg mixture, then coat with breadcrumbs, pressing crumbs firmly into sturgeon.

2. Heat oil in a large sauté pan over medium-high heat. When pan is very hot, add the sturgeon and sauté for 2 minutes on each side. Remove the sturgeon from the pan to paper towels, to absorb excess oil. Keep warm.

3. Drain the oil from the pan. Add butter and cook over high heat until it turns nut brown.

4. Put two slices of sturgeon on each of four warmed plates, and pour a portion of brown butter over each. Serve at once with lemon on the side.

Chicken and Kohlrabi Stew with Dumplings

This stew is a good example of what happens when the honest dishes of middle-class kitchens meet the refined cuisine of professional chefs.

Serves 10-12

Dumplings

1 pound skinless boneless chicken breasts

2 tablespoons fresh dill leaves

1 teaspoon salt

Freshly ground black pepper, to taste

2 egg whites

2 cups heavy (whipping) cream

Stew

1/2 cup (1 stick) unsalted butter

2/3 cup all-purpose flour

3 cups chicken stock

2 cups dry white wine

Salt and freshly ground pepper to taste

3 young kohlrabi (about 1 pound) peeled and sliced 1/2-inch thick

1 pound baby carrots, peeled and trimmed, or 1 pound regular carrots, peeled and cut into 1/2-inch diagonal pieces

2 chickens (3 pounds each), well-rinsed, patted dry, and cut into 8 pieces

To finish

3 quarts chicken stock

1/3 cup sugar

Juice of 2 lemons

1. To make the dumplings, place the chicken breasts, dill, salt, and pepper in a food processor. Process until finely minced, about 30 seconds. Add the egg whites and process again. With the machine running, slowly pour the heavy cream through the feed tube. As soon as the cream is added, turn off the machine. Transfer the mixture to a bowl; cover and chill for at least 4 hours, preferably overnight.

2. To start the stew, melt the butter in a nonreactive, very heavy, deep, large pot over medium heat. Add the flour and cook, stirring constantly with a wooden spoon until the roux turns a pale-blond color, about 5 minutes.

3. Add chicken stock and wine and bring to a boil, whisking constantly. Add a generous amount of salt and pepper, and reduce heat to low. Simmer, stirring occasionally, for 10 minutes.

4. Parboil the kohlrabi and carrots in a large pot of boiling salted water for 6 minutes. Drain, then rinse with cold water to stop the vegetables from cooking further.

5. Add the chicken pieces and parboiled vegetables to the stock mixture. Cover with a tight-fitting lid and simmer for 45 minutes.

6. Meanwhile, remove the dumpling batter from the refrigerator. Place the 3 quarts of chicken stock in a large wide pot, and bring to a boil over medium-high heat. Reduce heat to a simmer. Using two large soup spoons, make egg-shaped dumplings from the batter and drop them into the stock. Keep at a simmer, lowering the heat if necessary to prevent it from boiling. Simmer the dumplings until cooked through, 8 to 10 minutes. Remove with a slotted spoon and drain for a few seconds on a clean cloth towel or napkin.

7. Remove the stew from the heat. Add the dumplings and re-cover the pot.

To finish:

1. In a heavy skillet, heat the sugar until it melts and caramelizes, turning a golden brown color. As soon as it caramelizes, remove the pan from the heat and stir in the lemon juice. Take about 2 1/2 cups of stock from the stew and add to the skillet. Stir over medium heat until well blended, about 30 seconds.

2. Skim off any excess fat from the stew. Drizzle the sauce over the stew, stir, and return to the stove top; heat to a simmer.

Quail and Gin

Serves 3

1/2 cup (1 stick) plus 1 tablespoon unsalted butter

6 quail, partially boned, split, and flattened, giblets reserved (quail can be purchased this way at a butcher shop.)

1/4 cup all-purpose flour

Salt and pepper to taste

10 juniper berries, crushed

1/3 cup gin

2 tablespoons sour cream, at room temperature

1 teaspoon lingonberries (available in jars)

3 individual-sized brioche, sliced and toasted

1. In a medium-sized heavy skillet over high heat, melt the 1 tablespoon butter. Add the quail giblets and sauté until browned and cooked through. Coarsely chop the giblets and reserve.

2. In a large bowl, combine the flour, salt, and pepper. Dredge the split quail in the mixture, shaking off excess.

3. In a large nonreactive heavy skillet over medium-high heat, melt the remaining 1/2 cup butter. When the butter begins to bubble, add the quail in batches. Sauté until browned all over and the thigh meat is springy to the touch, about 7 minutes per batch. Return all the browned quail to the skillet.

4. Reduce the heat to medium and add the crushed juniper berries. Cover the pan and cook, stirring once, for 5 minutes.

5. Pour the gin over the quail and carefully ignite. Shake skillet gently until flames subside.

6. Reduce the heat to medium-low and simmer, uncovered, stirring often and basting with the pan juices, for 5 minutes.

7. Stir the sour cream into the pan juices, one teaspoon at a time. Then stir in the lingonberries until well blended. Season to taste with salt and pepper.

8. To serve, arrange the brioche toast on a serving plate, place a quail on top of each piece of brioche, and sprinkle with chopped giblets. Spoon pan juices over all.

Lamb and Duck Cassoulet with Lentils

Cassoulet was brought over from the Middle East, where it was originally made with chick-peas, lamb, and olive oil. When the Jews left Palestine in the Middle Ages, they brought this dish, served for the traditional Sabbath meal, with them to France. Its French name comes from *cassolo*, the earthenware casserole dish made in the town of Issel, near Castelnaudary. To simplify this recipe, instructions on making confit of goose and duck, traditionally part of cassoulet, were eliminated. The confit won't be missed.

Serves 10

1 pound lentils, soaked in cold water for an hour and drained

1 ounce olive oil

1 pound boneless lamb, cut in medium-size pieces

12 ounces boneless duck meat (leg and thigh is best), cut into medium-size pieces

Freshly ground black pepper

1 pound bacon, cut into 1-inch pieces

1 1/2 tablespoons finely chopped garlic

2 ripe red tomatoes, peeled, seeded, and coarsely chopped

1/2 cup tomato purée

1 onion, peeled and halved crosswise

4 bay leaves

6 cloves

Pinch of thyme

2 quarts rich beef stock

12 ounces garlic sausage, blanched and cut into 1/2-inch dice

Salt to taste

1 cup bread crumbs

4 tablespoons chopped fresh parley

4 tablespoons butter, melted

1. Put lentils in a large saucepan and cover with plenty of cold water.

2. Bring to a quick boil and cook over medium-high heat for 10 to 12 minutes, or until tender. Drain.

3. Heat oil in a large saucepan. When very hot, add the lamb.

4. Sear the lamb evenly on all sides, cooking for about 3 minutes.

5. Add the duck and continue to cook for another 3 to 5 minutes.

6. Season meats well with pepper. Add bacon to pan and stir well, then add garlic and cook for 5 minutes more. Stir in chopped tomatoes and tomato puree.

7. Stud the onion halves by attaching two bay leaves with three cloves to each. Add to saucepan; season with thyme, add stock, and bring to a boil.

8. Reduce heat, cover, and cook over medium heat for 1 1/4 hours, skimming off scum from time to time. Remove cover, stir in lentils, and continue slowly cooking the mixture, uncovered, for another 30 minutes. Remove studded onion halves and discard.

9. Add sausage and cook for additional 10 minutes. Season with salt and pepper.

10. In a small bowl, toss together bread crumbs and parsley.

11. To serve, ladle each portion of cassoulet into a shallow oven-proof earthenware dish approximately 1 1/2 inches deep, and lightly coat with bread crumbs.

12. Brush surface with a small amount of butter, and place under a preheated broiler for 3 minutes, or until golden brown. Serve at once.

Pot-au-Feu

George Lang says childhood returns to him with the arresting aroma of a pot-au-feu. Escoffier called it the symbol of family life, and Mirabeau, the eighteenth-century French revolutionary hero, went far out on a metaphoric limb to say: "In the common pot-au-feu lies the foundation of the Empire."

Serves 10

6 pounds short ribs of beef

3 pounds beef brisket

1 veal shank (about 3 pounds)

Coarse salt (kosher salt or sea salt)

1 spice bag containing 6 sprigs parsley, 1 sprig fresh thyme, 2 teaspoons cracked black peppercorns, and 1 bay leaf, wrapped in a double thickness of cheesecloth and tied with butcher's twine

1 onion, peeled and halved, each half studded with 2 cloves

3 pounds marrowbones, each cut to about 6-inch lengths and individually wrapped in cheesecloth with both ends tied

1 fowl weighing 3 to 4 pounds

10 small carrots, peeled and tied in a bunch

1 medium-size knob of celery, peeled and quartered

5 leeks, washed well to remove sand, trimmed, sliced in half lengthwise, and tied in a bunch

10 small turnips, peeled and trimmed

Freshly ground white pepper to taste

Table condiments

Coarse salt

Cornichons

Dijon mustard

Dark stone-ground mustard

Fresh Creamed Horseradish Sauce (*see* recipe page 156)

Toast for marrow

1. Put ribs, beef brisket, and veal shank in a deep soup pot; add salt and enough cold water to cover the meat (about 6 quarts). Bring to a simmer.

2. Add a few tablespoons of cold water to retard boiling in order to remove foam from the surface. Keep skimming as necessary.

3. Add spice bag and studded onion halves and simmer, uncovered, for about 2 hours.

4. Add marrowbones and fowl. Continue to simmer for 1 hour. Skim foam from time to time.

5. Add vegetables and simmer approximately 45 minutes more, removing each vegetable when it becomes tender (test by pricking with a fork).

6. Remove string from cooked vegetables, and keep them warm by putting in a small pot with some of the cooking stock. Do not place over direct heat or vegetables will overcook.

7. Remove meats from cooking stock and keep warm (as with vegetables).

8. Strain stock into another soup pot through moistened cheesecloth. Bring to a simmer. Skim off any fat, and season to taste with coarse salt and white pepper.

9. Discard spice bag and remove cheesecloth from marrowbones.

10. Remove chicken and reserve for another use (it can be the basis for a particularly flavorful chicken salad).

Setting the stage:

1. Put short ribs and veal shank on a heated oval platter with a lip.

2. Garnish by surrounding meats with vegetables. Arrange marrowbones on top.

3. Moisten entire platter with some of the simmering bouillon. Cover bouillon and keep hot.

To serve:

1. Serve bouillon in cups as a first course.

2. Serve thinly sliced hot toast and marrowbones along with individual marrow spoons. Coarse salt should be on the table.

3. Sliced brisket of beef and the short ribs are served with the vegetables as a separate course. Sauce and condiments are offered as an accompaniment.

Creamed Horseradish Sauce

6 tablespoons freshly grated (or bottled, drained and rinsed) horseradish

1 1/2 cups heavy cream

2 teaspoons Dijon mustard

2 tablespoons white wine vinegar

Pinch of salt

1. Combine all ingredients in a mixing bowl and blend well.

2. Adjust seasoning to taste with a bit more mustard or a pinch of salt. Serve at room temperature.

Sauerbraten Bohemian Style

After ordering this at the Café, a regular customer commented, "I am glad the Café des Artistes specializes in adult dishes."

Serves 8

Note: Meat must marinate for one week prior to cooking.

2 quarts apple cider

1 1/2 quarts apple cider vinegar

1 tablespoon juniper berries

8 bay leaves

4 whole cloves

10 black peppercorns

10 white peppercorns

1 piece of beef shoulder, about 3 pounds

1/4 cup flour

1/4 cup vegetable oil

Salt and pepper

1 cup chopped onion

1 cup chopped carrot

1 cup chopped celery root

1 tablespoon tomato paste

3 tablespoons Dijon mustard

2 quarts heavy cream

2 tablespoons sour cream

1/4 cup lingonberries (available in jars)

1. In a large, heavy, nonreactive saucepan, place the apple cider vinegar, 2 quarts water, juniper berries, bay leaves, cloves, and peppercorns. Bring to a boil and boil for 10 minutes. Let cool completely.

2. Place the meat in the cooled liquid and marinate, refrigerated, for one week. Turn meat over every day.

3. Remove meat from marinade (strain and reserve marinade) and dry with a clean towel. Season with salt and pepper, and roll in flour to coat completely. Preheat oven to 350 F.

4. Heat the oil in a heavy, large, flame-proof and ovenproof casserole (with a lid). Brown the meat on all sides. Add vegetables and sauté until caramelized.

5. Stir in strained marinade and tomato paste. Bring to a boil and cover. Braise in oven for 2 to 2 1/2 hours, or until meat is tender.

6. Remove meat from casserole and keep warm while you finish preparing the dish.

7. Bring liquid in the casserole to a boil and reduce volume by half. In a separate dish, combine the sour cream and heavy cream, then stir in a ladle of the hot liquid from the casserole to temper the cream. Pour cream mixture into the casserole, bring to a simmer, and reduce until liquid is a creamy consistency, at least 15 to 20 minutes. Strain.

8. Stir the mustard and lingonberries into the strained sauce. Return meat to the pot and bring to boil. Taste for seasoning and adjust if necessary.

9. Slice the sauerbraten and serve with the sauce ladled over the top.

Beef Cheeks with Creamed Spinach, Rösti Potatoes, and Apple-Horseradish Sauce

Serves 6

6 beef cheeks

2 Spanish onions, roughly chopped

3 cloves garlic, smashed

1 tablespoon salt

1 tablespoon black peppercorns

1 teaspoon dried thyme

2 bay leaves

3 carrots, roughly chopped

3 parsnips, roughly chopped

2 leeks, roughly chopped

1. In a heavy soup pot, combine the beef, onion, garlic, salt, peppercorns, thyme, and bay leaves. Add water to cover. Bring to a boil, then reduce heat and simmer for 1 hour.

2. Add carrots, parsnips, and leeks. Simmer for between a 1/2 hour and 1 hour, until beef cheeks are tender. Turn off heat, and let stand.

Rösti Potatoes

5 Idaho or russet potatoes

1 large Spanish onion, minced

1 tablespoon caraway seeds

Salt and pepper to taste

5 tablespoons olive oil

1. Boil potatoes until cooked but still firm. Cool, then peel. Grate potatoes coarsely. Mix with onion, caraway seeds, salt, and pepper.

2. Pour 3 tablespoons olive oil into a large, heavy, nonstick sauté pan and heat over medium heat. Add potato mixture and press down with a spatula to make a compressed cake shape. Cook until brown and crispy on the bottom, which should take several minutes. Turn the potato cake onto an inverted dinner plate. Pour remaining olive oil into the pan, then slide potato cake back into the pan on the uncooked side. Cook until underside is brown and crispy.

Creamed Spinach

1 pound fresh spinach

1 onion, minced

3 tablespoons butter

3 tablespoons all-purpose flour

1 teaspoon minced garlic

Salt and pepper to taste

Sprinkling of freshly grated nutmeg

1/2 cup heavy cream

1. Wash and blanch spinach. Squeeze out excess water and chop. Place spinach and a little of the cooking liquid in a blender and puree. Mixture should be on the loose side.

2. Sauté onion in butter until lightly browned. Sprinkle flour over the onion and stir, then cook for 1 minute.

3. Add pureed spinach, garlic, salt, pepper, and nutmeg. Stir and sauté for 2 minutes. Stir in heavy cream; sauté until smooth.

Apple-Horseradish Sauce

6 apples, peeled and cored

1 cup white wine

1 tablespoon lemon juice

1 cinnamon stick

1/4 teaspoon ground clove

1 tablespoon freshly grated horseradish, or to taste

1. Roughly chop four of the apples and place in a small, heavy saucepan. Add 1/2 cup water, white wine, lemon juice, cinnamon stick, and cloves. Bring to a boil, then reduce heat and simmer, uncovered, for 20 minutes, stirring occasionally. Let cool.

2. Grate remaining two apples. Add to the cooked apples, along with the horseradish. Adjust seasoning to taste.

Chive Sauce

3 pieces high-quality white bread, crusts removed

Milk

2 hard-boiled eggs, chopped

1/2 cup mayonnaise

1 tablespoon white vinegar

Salt and pepper to taste

2 tablespoons chopped chives

1. Place bread in a small bowl and cover with milk; soak for 20 minutes. Squeeze liquid out of bread (discard liquid), and put soaked bread in a food processor. Add hard-boiled eggs, mayonnaise, vinegar, salt, and pepper. Process until smooth.

2. Remove mixture from the processor and adjust seasoning, adding vinegar, salt, or pepper to taste. Add chopped chives.

To serve:

1. Remove beef cheeks from broth; trim fat if necessary. Slice cheeks thinly, and put slices into individual soup plates along with some of the vegetables (carrots, parsnips, and leeks). Ladle over a little warm broth.

2. Cut a wedge of the rösti potato cake and put on the rim of the soup plate.

3. Serve a dish of creamed spinach at the table, as well as the apple-horseradish and chive sauces.

Tripe aux Pruneaux

There is a secret brotherhood of tripe lovers, and they are just as misunderstood as the Rosicrucians were in the Middle Ages. This particular version is based on uncooked beef tripe, though ethnic Italian, French, and Portuguese butchers often sell it already cooked. Tripe, a texture food, is a perfect carrier of taste. The surprising combination in this recipe yields a sinewy, silky fusion of flavors and lip-smacking texture.

Serves 10

Note: Calves feet and tripe must soak overnight before cooking.

10 pounds calves' feet

6 pounds honeycomb tripe, cut into
   1 1/2-inch triangles

2 1/4 gallons unsalted beef stock

1 spice bag containing 10 bay leaves,
   8 black peppercorns, 6 parsley sprigs,
   6 whole cloves, 1 bulb garlic, halved,
   and 1 tablespoon dried thyme wrapped
   in a double thickness of cheesecloth
   and tied with butcher's twine

1 quart dry white wine

6 large carrots, peeled

2 large onions, peeled

1/4 cup tomato puree

1 cup chopped carrot

1 pound pitted prunes

1/4 cup Calvados or applejack

Salt and freshly ground pepper to taste

10 medium-sized potatoes, boiled and
   peeled

1. In two separate bowls, cover calves' feet and tripe with water and soak overnight in the refrigerator. Drain.

2. Preheat oven to 350 F.

3. In two separate large saucepans, blanch calves' feet and tripe in boiling salted water for 15 minutes. Drain.

4. Combine calves' feet, stock, wine, whole carrots, onions, tomato puree, and spice bag in a very large stockpot and bring to a rolling boil.

5. Remove from heat, cover with a tight-fitting lid, and put in the oven. Simmer for 5 hours.

6. Remove calves' feet. Add tripe to stockpot and return to oven to cook for 2 hours.

7. Remove carrots, onions, and spice bag; discard all. Add chopped carrots to pot and continue cooking for an additional 30 minutes.

8. When calves' feet are cool enough to handle, remove bones and discard. Cut tender skin and usable meat to 1/2-inch chunks.

9. Transfer stockpot to stove top. Using a strainer, remove tripe and chopped carrots to a bowl; keep warm. Cook stock over high heat until reduced to 8 cups, about 30 minutes. Reduce heat to medium. Add meats, chopped carrots, prunes, and Calvados. Cook 10 minutes. Taste and season with salt and pepper.

10. To serve, pour over potatoes in shallow soup bowls.

Salad of Brussels Sprout Leaves

Serves 4

30 ounces fresh brussels sprouts, trimmed, tough outer leaves removed

6 tablespoons extra-virgin olive oil

2 teaspoons minced garlic

1 tablespoon white wine vinegar

Salt and pepper to taste

1. Remove the leaves from the brussels sprouts, one by one, trimming the stem as you go so that the leaves separate from the stalk more easily. Rinse and pat dry.

2. In a wok or large heavy skillet over high heat, heat the olive oil. Add the brussels sprout leaves and garlic; stir-fry for 2 minutes.

3. Transfer the leaves to a salad bowl and toss with the vinegar; season with salt and pepper.

Ilona Torte

George Lang created this dish in 1969, naming it after his mother and daughter, and it is included in his *Cuisine of Hungary* (Atheneum 1971 and 1982). One slice will bring temporary happiness, which is more than we get from most things these days. According to fairly reliable sources, it also acts as an aphrodisiac, and quantities of the Ilona torte will turn a puny creature into a Casanova, or a woman you wouldn't notice on a desert island into Madame du Barry—both of whom, by the way, indulged in quantities of chocolate.

Serves 12 or more

5 ounces semisweet chocolate,
  cut into small pieces
1 cup sugar
6 tablespoons unsalted butter
8 eggs, separated
1 3/4 cup plus 1/3 cup coarsely ground walnuts

2 tablespoons fresh white bread crumbs
Pinch of salt
Butter
Flour
Mocha Butter Cream (*see* recipe page 163)
Walnut halves for garnish

1. Preheat oven to 375 F.

2. In a medium saucepan, combine chocolate and sugar with 1/4 cup water and cook over moderate heat for about 5 minutes, stirring occasionally, until mixture is smooth. Let cool for 15 minutes.

3. In a mixing bowl, beat butter until light and fluffy.

4. Add egg yolks one at a time, beating until each is incorporated.

5. Slowly beat in chocolate mixture until well blended. Then add 1 3/4 cups ground walnuts and bread crumbs, mixing just enough to combine thoroughly.

6. In a large mixing bowl, whip egg whites and salt until stiff peaks form.

7. Very gently fold egg whites into the chocolate mixture.

8. Lightly butter a 10-inch by 3-inch-deep torte pan Sprinkle with flour and shake out any excess.

9. Pour batter into pan and bake for 35 to 40 minutes. Let the cake cool in the pan for 15 minutes.

10. Invert torte onto a cooling rack and let cool completely.

11. Cut the cooled torte horizontally into two layers.

12. Place top half, topside down, on a round platter.

13. Cover the cake with 3/4 cup of Mocha Butter Cream, reserving 1 cup for decoration.

14. Place the second layer of cake on top of the filling, smooth side up.

15. Cover the top and sides of the cake with Mocha Butter Cream, using a flexible cake spatula.

16. Press the remaining 1/3 cup ground walnuts into the Mocha Butter Cream on the sides of the cake.

17. Using a pastry bag with a star tip, decorate the top edges and base of the cake with the reserved 1 cup of Mocha Butter Cream.

18. Garnish the top with walnut halves.

Mocha Butter Cream

6 ounces semisweet chocolate, cut into
  small pieces

2 teaspoons instant espresso powder

1 cup plus 2 tablespoons unsalted butter,
  at room temperature

3 egg yolks

2/3 cup confectioners' sugar

1. In a small saucepan, combine chocolate, 1/3 cup water, and espresso powder.

2. Stir over low heat until the chocolate is completely melted. Scrape into a bowl and let cool completely.

3. Using an electric mixer, cream butter until light and fluffy.

4. Add egg yolks one at a time, beating until each is incorporated.

5. Gradually add confectioners' sugar.

6. Scrape in chocolate mixture and blend thoroughly.

Orange Savarin

Leftover savarin should be sliced and toasted in a broiler, a perfect accompaniment for an afternoon tea. Credit goes to chef Michael Picciano, whose original formula was the basis for the Café's recipe. The creator of a new dish, just like the discoverer of an island, has the privilege of naming it. Stanislaus Leszczynski, king of Poland from 1704 to 1709, was an amateur baker who named his new dessert Ali Baba, after a character in his favorite book, *A Thousand and One Nights* (or *The Arabian Nights' Entertainments*). The famous Parisian *maître pâtissier* Julienne changed the recipe slightly and renamed it Savarin, after the famous French gastronome Brillat-Savarin.

Serves 18

1 1/2 cups unsalted butter, at room temperature

2 1/2 cups granulated sugar

8 large eggs, separated

2 1/4 teaspoons vanilla extract

Grated rind of 2 oranges (about 1 1/4 tablespoons)

2 1/4 cups sifted all-purpose flour

1/2 teaspoon baking soda

Strained juice of 2 oranges (about 1/2 cup)

1 1/2 teaspoons cream of tartar

1/4 teaspoon salt

2 to 3 tablespoons orange-flavored liqueur (optional)

1. Preheat oven to 325 F.

2. Butter and flour a 10-inch tube pan with a removable bottom.

3. Cream butter in the bowl of an electric mixer until fluffy. Gradually add 1 1/4 cups of the sugar; beat butter and sugar together until light and fluffy, about 3 minutes.

4. Add egg yolks one at a time, beating well after each addition. Add vanilla and orange rind and beat mixture at medium speed for 5 minutes, or until light and fluffy.

5. Sift flour and baking soda together. Add to creamed mixture in three parts, alternating with orange juice and beginning and ending with dry ingredients. Beat until smooth.

6. In another large bowl, beat egg whites with cream of tartar and salt until soft peaks form. Gradually add the remaining cup of sugar and beat at high speed until stiff peaks form. Gently fold into batter.

7. Pour batter into tube pan. Bake in the center of oven for 1 hour and 35 minutes, until the cake is golden and pulls away from the sides of the pan.

8. Remove cake pan to a wire rack. While the cake is still hot, brush with liqueur. Let cool 10 minutes, and then remove from pan.

9. To serve, cut into one-inch slices.

Buttermilk Pie

Through some inexplicable transformation, this late-eighteenth-century American pie will taste almost like a lemon cheesecake by the next day. The filling has only five simple ingredients, so it's rather difficult to explain why this pie affords such a feeling of sensuous luxury.

Serves 8

Dough

1 1/4 cups all-purpose flour

1/4 teaspoon salt

6 tablespoons very cold unsalted butter, cut
    into 6 pieces

2 tablespoons solid vegetable shortening

3 tablespoons ice-cold water

Filling

3 large eggs

1 cup granulated sugar

2 cups buttermilk

1 tablespoon fresh lemon juice

1 teaspoon vanilla extract

1. Sift flour, combine with salt, and put in the bowl of a food processor fitted with a metal chopping blade. Whirl for a few seconds to mix.

2. Sprinkle butter and shortening on top of flour. Process with pulsing action for about 10 seconds, until mixture resembles coarse oatmeal.

3. Sprinkle ice-cold water over mixture. Process with pulsing action for about 10 seconds, until mixture just begins to stick together but before a ball forms.

4. Shape dough into a ball, wrap in wax paper, and chill for 1 hour.

5. Preheat oven to 450 F.

6. Roll out the dough between sheets of lightly floured wax paper, then set into 9-inch pie plate. Trim and crimp to form a decorative edge. Chill until firm.

7. Set a square of wax paper inside the pie shell and fill with dried beans, rice, or pie weights.

8. Bake 10 to 12 minutes, until the dough looks set. Remove beans and wax paper.

9. Prick the dough with a fork, then continue baking for 10 minutes longer, until baked through.

10. Reduce oven temperature to 350 F.

11. Beat eggs in a large bowl. Beat in sugar, then add buttermilk, lemon juice, and vanilla extract and mix well. Pour into baked shell.

12. Bake 50 to 60 minutes, until filling is firm and knife inserted in the center comes out clean.

13. Serve slightly chilled, with whipped cream on the side.

Blueberry Shortcakes

Serves 6

2 cups all-purpose flour	1/2 cup unsalted butter
2 tablespoons sugar	1 egg, beaten
1 tablespoon baking powder	2/3 cup light cream
1/2 teaspoon salt	Blueberry Sorbet (*see* recipe below)

1. Sift together dry ingredients. Cut in butter until mixture resembles coarse crumbs.

2. Combine egg and cream. Add all at once to dry ingredients, stirring only to moisten.

3. Turn dough out onto floured surface; knead gently for about 30 seconds. Pat or roll dough until 1/2-inch thick. Cut six biscuits using floured 2-1/2-inch round or fluted cutter. Bake on ungreased baking sheet at 475 F for about 10 minutes, or until dry and cooked through.

Blueberry Sorbet

1 cup sugar	Juice of 3 lemons
1 cup water	2 cups whipped cream
4 pints blueberries	Confectioners' sugar

1. Put sugar and water into a small, heavy saucepan. Bring to a boil. Turn off heat and let cool (this is simple syrup).

2. Puree 3 1/2 pints of the blueberries with some of the simple syrup until sweetened to taste.

3. Strain mixture and add lemon. Reserve 3/4 cup of this mixture to use as blueberry coulis. Freeze the remainder in a sorbet machine or ice-cream maker.

To assemble:

To make each serving, split a shortcake lengthwise. Pour some blueberry coulis on a dessert plate. Set the bottom half of the shortcake in the coulis. Drop a spoonful of the whipped cream on the shortcake. Place one scoop of blueberry sorbet on the whipped cream. Garnish with fresh blueberries. Lean top half of shortcake against the sorbet. Sprinkle with confectioners' sugar.

Milchrahmstrudel

Strudel dough, also known as phyllo pastry, was brought to Hungary by the Turks in the sixteenth century. Member nations of the Austro-Hungarian Empire each created their own variation, with Milchrahmstrudel being the Viennese contribution.

Serves 12

3/4 pound day-old white bread or rolls,
  crusts removed, cut into cubes
  (about 6 cups)

2 cups milk

12 tablespoons (1 1/2 sticks) unsalted butter

1/3 cup confectioners' sugar

Zest of 1 lemon

1/8 teaspoon salt

5 eggs, separated

1/2 teaspoon vanilla extract

2 cups farmers cheese (3/4 pound)

3/4 cup sour cream

3/4 cup golden raisins

1/3 cup granulated sugar

4 ounces frozen phyllo dough (let stand
  unopened at room temperature for
  30 minutes before using)

1/4 cup melted butter

1. Pour 1 1/4 cups milk over the bread cubes, stir together, and let stand.

2. In a heavy-duty mixer, combine the 12 tablespoons butter, confectioners' sugar, lemon zest, and salt. Beat together until completely creamed, about 5 minutes. Add egg yolks and vanilla extract and beat for 3 more minutes. Add the soaked bread cubes, farmer's cheese, sour cream, and raisins. Mix for 3 more minutes.

3. In another bowl, beat egg whites with granulated sugar until mixture has the texture of shaving cream. Carefully fold the beaten egg whites into the cheese mixture.

4. Preheat oven to 325 F.

5. Butter a 9x12 glass or ceramic baking dish. Line the entire bottom of the baking dish with phyllo dough, brushing each piece with melted butter. Place overlapping pieces into the dish crosswise so that half of the dough is in the dish and half of the dough is outside the dish. Pour cheese mixture into the phyllo-lined dish. Fold phyllo from outside dish over top, then cover with another whole piece of phyllo dough. If there is any melted butter remaining, brush top with butter.

6. Bake for 20 minutes. In the meantime, heat remaining 3/4 cup milk until just before boiling point. After 20 minutes, carefully pour hot milk into the baking dish. Bake for 40 minutes more, or until top of Milchrahmstrudel is set. Let stand at room temperature for a half-hour before serving. Dust with confectioners' sugar if desired.

"It has been suggested that because the Café des Artistes is a restaurant we own, we therefore created the best restaurant we could. This kind of sentence irritates us no end. One doesn't do the best, or medium best, or worst. One does what one must. There is an ancient Greek word, *filotimo*, which is usually translated as love and honor. What it really means is to justify your life through your work. To be a restaurateur should mean being an honorable person who will really give value for the money. I think at the Café des Artistes we do that, all of us." —*George Lang*

At once innovative and traditional, the Café subtly reminds customers that, above all, fine dining should be enjoyable.

INDEX